Beyond the Beach Blanket

A Field Guide to
Southern California Coastal Wildlife

Marina Curtis Tidwell

2005
Mountain Press Publishing Company
Missoula, Montana

Library of Congress Cataloging-in-Publication Data

Tidwell, Marina Curtis, 1955-
  Beyond the beach blanket : a field guide to southern California
coastal wildlife / Marina Curtis Tidwell.
    p. cm.
Includes bibliographical references and index.
ISBN 0-87842-506-3 (pbk. : alk. paper)
  1. Coastal animals—California, Southern—Identification. I. Title.
QL164.T53 2005
591.75'1'097949—dc22
                                                        2005003068

PRINTED IN HONG KONG
BY MANTEC PRODUCTION COMPANY

Mountain Press Publishing Company
P.O. Box 2399 • Missoula, Montana 59806
(406) 728-1900

To my grandmother,
Gertrude Bastion Francis,
who loves all creatures
great and small

Contents

PREFACE   *viii*

ACKNOWLEDGMENTS   *ix*

INTRODUCTION   *1*

How to Use This Book   *3*

Human Impacts   *6*

Beachcombing and Collecting   *7*

Important Things to Know about the Beach   *8*

Phylums Discussed in This Book   *11*

How to Tell Shells Apart   *12*

   Terms Used to Describe Bivalves   *13*

   Terms Used to Describe Gastropods   *13*

Things to Bring   *15*

SANDY BEACHES   *16*

Mollusks   *18*

   Sand-Dwelling Bivalves (Clams and Mussels)   *18*

   Free-Swimming Bivalves (Scallops)   *42*

   Gastropods (Snails)   *46*

Echinoderms   *52*

   Sand Dollar   *52*

Arthropods   *54*

   Crabs   *54*

Cnidarians   *58*

   Hydroids   *58*

Mini Habitat   *60*

   Brown Algae or Kelp   *60*

   Parts of Kelp   *62*

   Wildlife on Kelp   *64*

ROCKY SHORES   70

Mollusks   72
  Rock-Dwelling Bivalves (Mussels, Oysters, Piddocks)   72
  Polyplacophora (Chitons)   80
  Flat-Shelled Gastropods (Snails)   82
  Spiral-Shelled Gastropods (Snails)   94
  Mollusks without Shells (Sea Slugs and Octopus)   108

Cnidarians   114
  Anemones   114

Annelids   118
  Tube-Building Marine Worms   118

Arthropods   120
  Barnacles   120
  Isopods   124
  Hermit Crabs   126
  True Crabs   128

Echinoderms   130
  Sea Stars   130
  Sea Urchins   132
  Sea Cucumbers   134

Chordates   136
  Bony Fish   136

NEARSHORE WATERS   140

Plankton   142
  Phytoplankton   142
  Red Tides   144
  Tunicates   146

Cnidarians   148
  Jellies   148

Arthropods   152
  Lobsters and Crabs   152

Chordates   154
  Bony Fish   154
  Cartilaginous Fish (Rays and Sharks)   166

Marine Mammals   *174*
  Sea Lions   174
  Seals   176
  Dolphins   178
  Gray Whale   184

BIRDS   *188*

Nearshore Birds   *190*
  Gulls   190
  Terns   196
  Skimmer   200
  Pelicans   202
  Cormorant   206

Birds of Rocky Shores   *208*
  Oystercatchers   208
  Sandpipers   208

Birds of Sandy Beaches   *210*
  Sandpipers   210

Birds of Coastal Wetlands   *216*
  Sandpipers   216
  Plovers   218
  Grebes   220
  Herons and Egrets   222
  Ducks   226
  Raptors   228
  Rail   230
  Sparrow   232

RESOURCES   *235*

SELECTED BIBLIOGRAPHY   *238*

INDEX   *243*

Preface

Mmm, the beach. Blues skies, balmy winds, sun-dappled waves lapping at your feet. Overhead the sun is like a yellow balloon tethered to the sky.

Why do we feel so rejuvenated after a day at the beach? After all, we can go to a pool and bask in the sun. It's just not the same, though, is it?

At the beach, we lie warmed and protected on the sand, dwarfed by the huge arc of sky. At the beach, the roar of the waves dulls our hearing. It is a sound that wipes out all sound—even our own incessant inner monologue. At the beach, we are aware, on some level, of the life teeming around us. The wilderness is there, just beyond the beach blanket, right at the tips of our toes. It seeps into our subconsciousness—the eternity, the silent, secret busy-ness of it all. So let's get up off the beach blanket and take a little walk on the wild side . . .

Acknowledgments

Many people lent me their expertise, especially Professor Genevieve Anderson of Santa Barbara City College; Herb Clarke, photographer and writer; Bill Rudman of Sea Slug Forum; and Carol Young, marine biology teacher and Monterey Bay Aquarium docent. In addition, I am deeply grateful to Heal the Bay for the opportunity to photograph live, underwater, rocky shore creatures at the Santa Monica Bay Aquarium; the Cabrillo Marine Aquarium for hours of pleasurable learning; and the many recreational anglers who told me their fish stories and let me photograph their catches.

Carolyn Allen of SunshinebyDesign.com provided the impetus and expert advice to begin the book. My editor at Mountain Press, James Lainsbury, was amazing and helped me take it to a whole new level. I'm very grateful for my sons' input: Tom for his help in choosing photos, Ted for his feedback on the text, and Colin for his curiosity and good humor on our many field trips. Most of all, I am thankful for my mother, Constance Curtis, and my husband, Robert Tidwell, without whose help and support this book could not have been completed.

SANTA BARBARA
COUNTY

Point
Conception

Santa
Barbara

VENTURA
COUNTY

LOS ANGELES
COUNTY

Carpinteria State Beach

Emma Wood State Beach

Ventura Harbor

Channel Islands

Malibu

Santa Monica State Beach

Venice Beach

Palos Verdes Peninsula

ORANGE
COUNTY

Bolsa Chica State Beach

Dana Point

SAN DIEGO
COUNTY

Santa Catalina

north county lagoons

San
Diego

La
Jolla

N

Point Loma

Sweetwater Marsh National Wildlife Refuge

California Bight
map not to scale

MEXICO

Introduction

Surrounded by mountains and edged by the blue Pacific Ocean, Southern California is composed of many different types of natural terrain. Besides forests, deserts, creeks, and wetlands, it has more than 350 miles of spectacular coastline. The deep eastward curve south of Point Conception has created a coastline that is noticeably different from that of northern California. The land is a coastal desert—a place where hot, dry air mingles with breezes and fog blowing in from the ocean. The sea here is known as the California Bight, and here southern currents drift up the coast from Mexico and mix with cold northern waters rounding the bend at Point Conception.

This embayment offers us many environments where we can encounter wildlife. From Palos Verdes Peninsula, Dana Point, and Point Loma, shoulders of land that jut into the Pacific, we can watch whales

Palos Verdes bluffs

1

San Pedro

migrate annually. Below these bluffs lie rocky beaches, coves, and tide-pools. Ribbons of sand, miles long and interspersed with small rocky outcroppings, stretch between enormous cliffs. These sandy beaches are among the most famous in the world: Malibu, Venice, Huntington, San Diego.

From Santa Barbara's superb south-facing shores to Coronado's spectacular white sands near the Mexican border, people flock to the coast to swim, sun, surf, and shop. Many Southern California dune areas were paved over and turned into quaint shopping areas, luxury homes, and resort hotels long ago. Marinas and wharves dock pleasure craft and small fishing boats, and long piers have been built out over the water for fishing, dining, and entertainment. With all this activity, it is easy to lose sight of the fact that beaches are still wildernesses—even where greatly urbanized. All sorts of uniquely adapted creatures live, breed, and raise their young in the coastal environment. It is easy to forget that our industries, recreational pursuits, and even our health depend on the well-being of these creatures and their habitats.

I hope that *Beyond the Beach Blanket* will enable you to see the beach differently. By learning to identify some of Southern California's common coastal animals and learning about their life cycles and the contribution that wildlife makes to a healthy coastal environment, I hope you will appreciate the beach and its life even more. Maybe this book will awaken even greater curiosity in you and inspire you to observe animal behavior whenever possible, go to a museum or aquarium, explore coastal wildlife through other books and Internet resources, become active in a conservation organization, or participate in beach cleanup days. Taking the time to appreciate the animals that depend on the coastal wilderness can enhance our leisure time, and also leave us renewed and filled with wonder.

How to Use This Book

I grouped most of the animals in this book according to habitat for two reasons. First, each creature is uniquely adapted to a particular niche—clams burrow, scallops swim, oysters bed, and so on. Most species found washed up on the shore of sandy beaches don't live in tidepools or on rocky shores. It's not that beachcombers never find a barnacle, chiton, or sea star on a sandy beach—or a sand crab or sand dollar on a rocky one—it's just that it is unlikely. By and large, the majority of seashells and exoskeletons of marine creatures that people find occur near, or in, the habitat those creatures lived in.

The second reason is that grouping by common habitat helps tell the story of interconnectedness. This organization takes into consideration that particular animals compete, breed, eat, live, and die in the same environment, sometimes within the same few inches of sand and water. Because the organization of this book mirrors real life, it should be easy to use. Merely flip through the section of the book that matches the beach habitat where you observed a particular shell or creature. Birds, of course, by virtue of their mobility, are an exception. I included them in a chapter of their own.

The Sandy Beaches chapter covers creatures, such as clams and other bivalves, sand dollars, and sand crabs, commonly found washed ashore along the open coast or on the shores of protected bays; this chapter also includes wildlife found in the small kelp wrack habitat.

The Rocky Shores chapter contains wildlife found in tidepools and on man-made structures such as breakwaters and pilings. Creatures include bedding and boring bivalves, chitons, rock-dwelling gastropods, barnacles, octopuses, sea slugs, marine worms, sea stars, anemones, crabs, urchins, and tidepool fish.

The Nearshore Waters chapter includes oceanic creatures great and small, including plankton, whales, jellies, fish, sharks, and more. Some

Sequit Point at Leo Carrillo State Beach in Malibu

Nearshore waters at Santa Monica State Beach

Emma Wood State Beach in Ventura

of these animals find shelter and food among the rocks or kelp beds in the nearshore waters. Others, such as the Guitarfish, live along sandy bottoms; and still others are pelagic (oceangoing), such as whales, but they arrive in Southern California's nearshore waters at certain times of the year.

The Birds chapter focuses on common species such as gulls, coastal wetland birds like egrets and grebes, and a few endangered species.

Scientists have devised a classification system for all living things, starting at the kingdom level and ending at the species and subspecies level. It helps them describe and learn about the world, and it can help us. I start each chapter with the most common phylum (or large group) of creatures found in the habitat. Within each phylum, I grouped animals by family, starting with the most common animals and ending with the least common—though of course judging what is common is somewhat subjective. I omitted scientific family names, which are unfamiliar to most people; instead I included common family names. For example, I used *clams* in place of Tellinidae and Veneridae, and *hermit crabs* in place of Diogenidae and Paguridae. This should make it easy for you to find related species in different chapters.

I also included the common and scientific name of each species. Scientific names are generally accepted throughout the world as the official name of a particular species. Common species names are often regional; I used the ones you are most likely to hear in Southern California. Although I profiled a few rare and endangered species, I made no attempt to include all of Southern California's coastal wildlife species. There are thousands of coastal marine species; I included the most common creatures—ones that you can easily observe with a little patience, and maybe a little luck!

Human Impacts

Wildlife can be injured by garbage, such as plastic bags, balloons, and Styrofoam; these objects can strangle animals or block their digestive systems, causing starvation. Strands of plastic, string, ribbon, and

Litter from city streets travels to the beach through storm-drain systems.

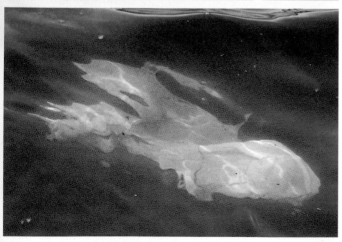

Plastic grocery bags look like jellies and are a threat to wildlife that eat them.

six-pack plastic rings can horribly injure animals as well. As a creature maneuvers through polluted water, these items can entangle a body part and act as a tourniquet or cut into the animal's skin. Many animals die from the resulting infection and gangrene. Rescue centers have their hands and facilities full trying to help animals that have been injured by trash.

Although environmental problems may seem overwhelming, beach-goers can help make a difference by taking a few simple actions:

- Don't leave behind picnic items, toys, fishing equipment, or garbage. Be a Good Samaritan and pick up after others as well.

- At home, be mindful of things that might end up in the gutter. The vast majority of trash on Southern California's beaches is street litter from inland areas that ends up in the gutter and is washed down storm drains to the beach. Rainwater also carries lawn and garden pesticides, pet fecal matter, and chemicals from cars through storm drains to the beach, where they harm coastal wildlife.

- Participate in beach cleanup days; major ones are held on Earth Day in April, and on Coastal Cleanup Day in September.

- Become active in a conservation organization. There are many to choose from and all of them welcome members and volunteers.

Beachcombing and Collecting

Some people enjoy the beach so much that they want to take part of it home with them. The best way to remember the beach is to bring your camera and take pictures, not animals! If you do collect shells, select just a few for your collection; leave the rest as shelters for small marine creatures.

You can learn a lot about animals by touching them, but do not pry them off their rocks—this can injure them. Creatures that can be easily picked up, such as sand crabs, should be handled briefly and gently. When you are done looking at them, return them where you found them. To protect animals, use the "one-finger rule" when handling them: touch them lightly with one finger. When exploring tidepools, lift and replace rocks carefully, and step lightly.

It's important to read and follow signs that are posted on the beach. In all tidepool areas, taking live animals is against the law, and some Southern California beaches are designated marine reserves where collecting of any kind—even shells, pebbles, or driftwood—is prohibited and punishable by heavy fines. The restrictions are meant to safeguard fragile habitats. Although you may only wish to collect one or two objects, the impact of this is huge when you consider how many people visit Southern California beaches every year.

Mollusks like clams and mussels are important to the seafood industry, but because of pollution and natural toxins from the periodic overgrowth of algae there are strict laws regulating the harvesting of all bivalves in order to keep consumers from being poisoned. Before you go clamming on one of Southern California's beaches, be sure you know the rules.

Important Things to Know about the Beach

Since there are more discoveries to be made when the tide is low, it's useful to check the tide table in the weather section of the local newspaper.

Date	Time/Height	Time/Height	Time/Height	Time/Height
May 1	5:15 AM/4.9 H	12:30 PM/-.9 L	6:30 PM/3 H	11:15 PM/2.0 L

The heights of the tides are measured in feet above and below the average low tide line, which is considered 0 feet. Tide height varies based on the moon cycle, but there usually are two high tides and two low tides every twenty-four hours along the Pacific coast. On the tide table above, the highest tide on May 1 would occur at 5:15 AM, and the lowest tide would occur at 12:30 PM. This low tide is considered a minus tide because it is less than the average low tide. Minus tides are especially fruitful times to visit the beach since more intertidal marine life is exposed. The tide cycle advances roughly fifty minutes per day, so on May 2, the lowest tide—based on the table above—would occur around 1:20 PM. For the most fruitful exploration, arrive at the beach one to two hours before low tide, and remember, the lower the tide, the more intertidal sands or rocks there will be exposed.

Marine organisms occupy almost the entire intertidal zone, which encompasses the section of beach between high and low tide. This area is in constant flux as tides cycle in and out. Animals that live in the intertidal zone are adapted to a constantly changing environment, but further out is the subtidal zone—the threshold of the deeper sea—which is more stable because it is not exposed by even the lowest minus tide. Most of the animals that you will be able to see on the beach live in the intertidal zone.

Check with a lifeguard before entering the water to swim or explore, especially if you are new to the Pacific coast. Many areas in Southern California have treacherous crosscurrents and undertows that

High tide makes it nearly impossible to explore the intertidal zone.

The same area at low tide reveals a tranquil tidepool.

can surprise and overpower even the strongest swimmers. A lifeguard can tell you current conditions, what to watch for, and whether the tide is coming in or going out—important information to know so a rising tide does not overwhelm you. Lifeguards do a great job of protecting people, but we have to do our part, too, by staying informed and following their advice.

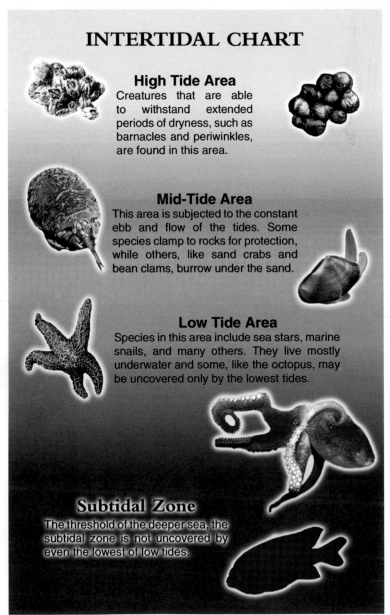

INTERTIDAL CHART

High Tide Area
Creatures that are able to withstand extended periods of dryness, such as barnacles and periwinkles, are found in this area.

Mid-Tide Area
This area is subjected to the constant ebb and flow of the tides. Some species clamp to rocks for protection, while others, like sand crabs and bean clams, burrow under the sand.

Low Tide Area
Species in this area include sea stars, marine snails, and many others. They live mostly underwater and some, like the octopus, may be uncovered only by the lowest tides.

Subtidal Zone
The threshold of the deeper sea, the subtidal zone is not uncovered by even the lowest of low tides.

Phylums Discussed in This Book
ARTHROPODS

The arthropod phylum is a large classification that includes insects and arachnids. Its name is derived from the Greek *arthro* for "jointed" and *pod* for "leg," and the phylum is composed of creatures that have jointed legs and hard external shells called *exoskeletons*. Crabs, isopods, barnacles, and lobsters are members of a specialized marine branch of arthropods called *crustaceans*. Most crustaceans are found on rocky shores and in the ocean; only a few have adapted to living on sandy beaches.

CHORDATES

The huge chordate phylum encompasses all animals with internal skeletons and backbones that encase spinal cords. Major divisions include mammals, birds, and fish. The Pacific Ocean contains thousands of fish species, and along Southern California some find shelter along rocky shores, especially where there are kelp beds or sea grasses to hide in. During low tide, the fish retreat to the subtidal zone, but they may also be found in isolated tidepools in the intertidal zone. The fish in this book can be divided into two classes: those with bony skeletons (Osteichthyes), and those with skeletons made of cartilage (Chondrichthyes). Sharks and rays belong to the latter class. Seals and sea lions, which come ashore to rest and give birth, and dolphins and whales, which are wholly aquatic, are mammals that are specifically adapted to the marine environment. They live in or migrate through Southern California's coastal waters.

CNIDARIANS

Cnidarians have radially symmetrical bodies around a central mouth, which is usually surrounded by tentacles. The tentacles are equipped with stinging cells called *nematocysts* that capture prey. Creatures in this phylum have two body forms; some of them live their entire life in one form, while others take on both forms at different stages in their life cycle. In the polyp stage a cnidarian is plantlike, like anemones and hydroids. It attaches to a substrate and extends its mouth upward, and it usually is not very mobile. A jelly spends most of its life in the medusa stage, floating freely through the water with its mouth hanging down from a gelatinous bell or dome. Some jellies live in our nearshore waters year-round; others live out at sea and are only driven ashore by seasonal winds and currents.

ECHINODERMS

Echinoderm means "spiny skin." All members of this phylum are covered with hard, protective plates. Though some echinoderm groups look very different from one another, all echinoderms have a circular body plan and body sections, such as arms, that radiate from a central point. This body structure is most obvious in sea stars, but it is also true of other echinoderms, such as sea urchins and sea cucumbers. The sand dollar is the only echinoderm that lives exclusively in a sandy habitat.

MOLLUSKS

The soft-bodied invertebrates of the mollusk phylum do not have an internal skeleton. They usually have some sort of protective shell, though shell-less sea slugs and octopuses are also members of this phylum. Mollusks have several major divisions, two of which are shell type: *bivalves,* meaning "two shells," and *univalves,* meaning "one shell." Univalves are commonly called *gastropods* or *marine snails.* Both bivalves and univalves come in many shapes, colors, and sizes, and they have adapted to many different marine environments. On sandy beaches, the majority of mollusks are bivalves, while gastropods are more common on rocky shores.

How to Tell Shells Apart

Many shells on the beach are difficult to tell apart. To identify some shells, you have to look at them very closely and you need to know how to identify certain characteristics. I use very little technical jargon in this book, but it is impossible to talk about marine wildlife without using some of that language. The pictures and definitions below will help you better understand marine wildlife that I discuss throughout this book. Another thing to keep in mind: all sizes I list in this book are approximations based on my field observations, personal collection, and reference books. Many reference books give maximum size, which is like describing an average human's height as that of a basketball player's; so in some cases, I listed a smaller size that, in my experience, is more common.

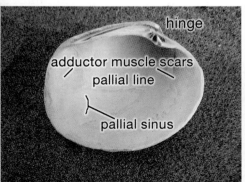

The interior and exterior of a Rough-Sided Littleneck (Protothaca laciniata) *shell*

TERMS USED TO DESCRIBE BIVALVES

adductor muscles. Muscles that close valves (shells). The muscles leave oblong, leaf-shaped "scars" on a shell's interior.

bands. Concentric lines, grooves, ridges, or colors on the exterior of a bivalve that parallel the bivalve's hinge. Bands represent the growth plane of a bivalve.

hinge. Where shells are connected. The tissue at the hinge becomes dry and brittle when an animal dies, and the shells separate.

mantle. A membrane between a mollusk's body and its shell. All shelled mollusks have a mantle, which secretes minerals to create their shells.

pallial line. The thin line on a shell's interior that runs between the adductor muscle scars. It indicates where the mantle muscle was attached.

pallial sinus. An indentation that occurs where the muscles that retracted the siphon were attached; where the pallial line makes an inward curve.

periostracum. A thin skinlike covering on the outside of some shells. It protects the shell from abrasion.

rays. Lines, grooves, ridges, or colors on the exterior of a bivalve that run perpendicular from the hinge to the edge of the shell.

TERMS USED TO DESCRIBE GASTROPODS

aperture. The opening in the shell where a snail's head and foot come out.

axis. The central internal "line" from the top spire to the base of the shell. Whorls spiral around the axis.

operculum. The small disk that is attached to the top of the snail's foot. It seals the shells aperture after the snail has pulled into its shell. Each species has a distinctive operculum.

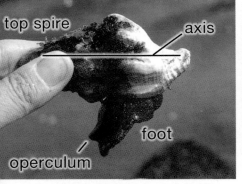

A live Kellet's Whelk (Kelletia kelleti)

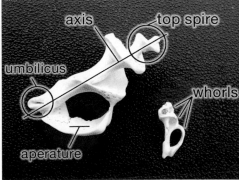

A fragment of a Kellet's Whelk

top spire. The whorls at the top of the axis. A snail's shell starts growing from the top spire, spiraling around the axis.

umbilicus. A hole in the axis located next to the aperture. In some species the hole is covered by shell.

varix. A swelling or rib that runs parallel to the axis of a shell, across the whorls. Some snails develop varices when they pause their growth.

whorls. The coiled part of the shell.

California Frog Shells (Bursa californica)

Things to Bring

- Sunblock, hat, and sunglasses
- A hand lens or magnifying glass
- Binoculars
- Pad and pencil for nature notes
- A camera to record, remember, and share your trip
- And of course a beach blanket and this book!

Sandy Beaches

At first sight, sandy beaches seem to be nothing more than sea, sky, and sand. A lot of pleasure can be found in the elemental sweep, the seeming barrenness of these beaches, especially after a busy, high-velocity workweek. Take the time to relax and let the simplicity of it seep into your heart, and then get ready for some surprises.

There is a great deal of wildlife uniquely adapted to living beneath the sand along the surf. The most common creatures are members of the mollusk phylum—soft-bodied creatures that usually have some sort of protective shell. Most of the seashells that wash up on sandy beaches come from bivalves, mollusks that spent their lives burrowed in sand or mud under the waves near the shore.

The types of invertebrates you find on a beach depend on geological features above and below the water. Some beaches have a gradual slope, and shallow waters continue up the beach past the breakers. You will find a wide variety of sand dwellers on this type of beach, such as clams, sand crabs, and sand dollars. Subtidal terrain that contains shell fragments and pebbles normally has the Pearly Jingle (*Anomia peruviana*) and Hemphill's Lima (*Lima hemphilli*). Muddy substrates will have *Chione* species of clams and slippersnails. Beaches that are shielded by a curve of land or man-made breakwaters have different varieties of wildlife than those that experience the full brunt of the Pacific Ocean. Coastal wetlands, a blanket term for lagoons, salt marshes, and estuaries, are other sandy beach habitats that are rich in wildlife. The salty water in coastal wetlands rises and falls with the high and low tides through some sort of outlet to the ocean, but these areas have few or no waves.

Beachcombing is especially rewarding when the tide is low because a long stretch of intertidal sand is exposed. When the tide is rising, look along the high tide line for shells, and be sure to look closely at any seaweed that is washed ashore—there is always something to see.

Santa Monica State Beach

Tide information and warnings on a lifeguard tower

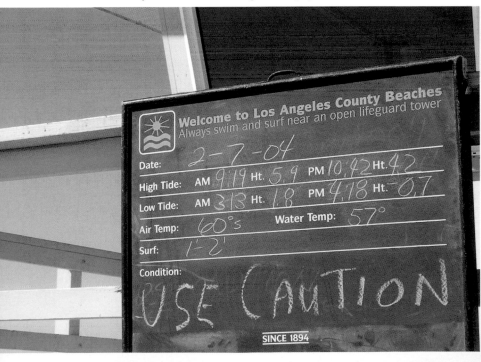

Mollusks

SAND-DWELLING BIVALVES (CLAMS AND MUSSELS)

Most of the bivalves that are adapted to sandy beaches are clams that usually remain hidden in the sand. A clam burrows by backing down into the sand: it extends its foot, wriggles it into the sand, and then draws its shell into the space the foot created. To climb up the burrow, a clam pushes against the walls with its foot and shoves its shell upward. Some species expel water between their halves; the water jets out around a clam's foot or siphons, propelling it forward. From the safety of its burrow, a sand-dwelling clam extends its siphon (one or two "tubes" depending on the species) above the sand to suck in food and water. Most clams have a retractable foot and siphon so these soft parts can be encased in a hard shell for protection.

Bean Clams (*Donax* species)

Up and down the coast of Southern California, thousands of tiny, ½- to 1-inch-long bean clams (*Donax* species) burrow into the sand at the water's edge. At high tide, this is the gravel you feel when walking into the water on a seemingly smooth sandy beach. At low tide, especially in spring and early summer when bean clams undergo a population explosion, they make a rough, colorful, pebbly-feeling carpet at the water's edge. Countless more have burrowed just an inch or so under the sand, and if you dig a little, you may find handfuls of them. Some people use the common name bean clam when referring to any number of small, young clams of different species, but a true *Donax* species has a distinct wedge shape, a glossy exterior, and a shell with colorful stripes and rays.

Unlike most other bivalves, it is possible to observe bean clams in action because they live at the surf line. If you take a handful of water and drip it over one, a delicate undulating foot may emerge from the thin slit between the colorful shells, or the translucent siphons may peep out—tubular organs that take in food and expel wastes. When a wave washes in, a few bean clams release from the sand while others tumble freely in the clear water; others dig in a little deeper and nestle together while their shells gently knock against their neighbors. One of them may shrug a little, like a deep sleeper under a blanket; another will put out a foot and begin to dig into the wet sand, or the siphons will emerge as it searches for food. It may even spit at you! A tiny "pfft!" will sparkle in the air for a brief second as it slams its shells shut.

*Live bean clams (*Donax *species)*

Bean clams have two flexible siphons and a large muscular foot.

A carpet of siphons

It is amazing how many different behaviors these clams exhibit. Watching live bean clams is especially rewarding because their behavior is representative of clams in general. Unfortunately, other clams live buried deeply in sand or far out in the intertidal zone, so that our only experience of them is finding their empty shells washed ashore.

Nuttall's Clam (*Nuttallia nuttallii*)
Sunset Clam (*Gari californica*)

Clams are awesome creatures—some can live as long as thirty years and a full-grown clam can filter up to ½ gallon of water an hour, removing and eating microscopic debris from thousands of gallons of ocean water every year. When this number is multiplied by thousands of species and billions of individual clams, you get an idea of the amazing role these creatures play in keeping the earth's shores clean.

After bean clams, the 4-inch-long Nuttall's Clam (*Nuttallia nuttallii*) and 3-inch-long Sunset Clam (*Gari californica*) are two of the more colorful bivalves you will find on Southern California beaches, and they are indicators of the large-scale coastal terrain. Since Nuttall's Clams are specifically adapted to areas with low waves, their presence indicates that the beach must be part of a protected bay where a curve of land or a man-made structure offers the clams protection. Sunset Clams are adapted to open shores as well as shielded areas.

Some Nuttall's Clams are very distinctive—purple inside and out; however, there is a great deal of variation in shell color, and a lighter-colored one may be mistaken for a macoma, since they both have smooth, glossy shells. Nuttall's do have some brown, tan, or purple on them, and their shells are more evenly curved, lacking the shape idiosyncrasies of macomas. These creatures were named after the great nineteenth-century naturalist Thomas Nuttall, the first European to classify many of California's birds, plants, and shells. There are a number of species named after him, indicating the breadth of his work and how he influenced and inspired other naturalists.

Sunset Clams are named for the pink rays that stripe their smooth white shells. When glistening with water they are breathtaking; unfortunately, like most shells, they fade as they dry. If you collect a Sunset Clam, try rubbing the shell with baby oil to maintain some of its luster and color.

Nuttall's Clam (Nuttallia nuttallii) *color variations*

Sunset Clam (Gari californica)

Indented Macoma (*Macoma indentata*)
Bent-Nose Macoma (*Macoma nasuta*)
White Sand Macoma (*Macoma secta*)
Pacific Grooved Macoma (*Leporimetis obesa*)

Most macoma clams are smooth, white, and glossy, and they have thin to paper-thin shells. They are 3 to 4 inches long, somewhat flat, and each one has a distinctive twist in its shell. For example, the Indented Macoma (*Macoma indentata*) has a subtle inward curve along one edge of its shell, and bands of growth rings that follow and emphasize the sculpting of this edge. If you hold a Bent-Nose Macoma (*Macoma nasuta*) upright on its rounder edge, you can see that the pointed tip of the shell bends to the right or the left, depending on which way you have the shell turned. This species is named for the odd bend; under the sand, it lies on its side with its "nose" pointing up. The bend in the shell allows the siphons to reach the surface so the clam can feed. The White Sand Macoma (*Macoma secta*) has a narrow, beveled ray that extends from its hinge to the edge of the shell, and one valve is much flatter and more delicate than the other. No matter what the twist, these macomas have glossy shells that retain their luster even when they are dry.

On the other hand, the Pacific Grooved Macoma (*Leporimetis obesa*) has a heavier, chalky shell, which is similar to a Venus clam's shell. These macomas are easy to identify though: just look for a white shell with a wavy, grooved ray on one side (like the White Sand Macoma's, but more obvious), then flip it over to check for a pale yellow interior.

Intact bivalves of all species are commonly called *butterfly shells* because the halves look like spread wings. Beachcombers love to find butterfly shells, but once the tissue that connects the hinge dries out, the shells usually separate. Storing a butterfly shell flat and placing a drop of white glue on its hinge will help keep the two halves together.

Top: *Indented Macoma* (Macoma indentata) Middle: *Bent-Nose Macoma*
(Macoma nasuta) Bottom: *White Sand Macoma* (Macoma secta)

One valve of the White Sand Macoma
is much flatter than the other.

The shell of a Bent-Nose
Macoma bends to the right.

Pacific Grooved Macoma (Leporimetis obesa)

California Jackknife (*Tagelus californianus*)
Rosy Jackknife (*Solen rostriformis*)
Purplish Tagelus (*Tagelus divisus*)
Bodega Tellin (*Tellina bodegensis*)

At low tide, the shallow waters of bays and coastal wetlands are dotted with the small, strange wormlike siphons of the 5-inch-long California Jackknife (*Tagelus californianus*), also called *California Tagelus,* protruding from holes in the muddy sand. These bivalves sit vertically in the mud with just the tips of their shells and siphons peeking out, pulling plankton, plant and animal detritus, and spawn from the water. The shells themselves are easy to recognize; they are white, rectangular, and have a central hinge. Sometimes people mistake the California Jackknife for the Rosy Jackknife (*Solen rostriformis*), a 3-inch-long clam that is also rectangular. Both species look something like an old-fashioned shaving razor. The Rosy Jackknife's hinge is on one corner of its shell, whereas the California Jackknife and Purplish Tagelus (*Tagelus divisus*) have centralized hinges. The Rosy Jackknife's pink and tan shell is very thin and delicate, and it is an uncommon species, so undamaged shells are rare. The streamlined shape of both of these clams helps them disappear rapidly into their burrows.

The 1½-inch-long Purplish Tagelus, an accidental transplant from the Atlantic Ocean, is becoming relatively common, probably because it is very adaptable and can live on any beach that has muddy sand. Its shells can be as thin and translucent as a fingernail, but they are sturdy enough to survive the pounding waves while other shells are broken into fragments.

The Bodega Tellin (*Tellina bodegensis*) has very thin shells that are glossy white and similar to the White Sand Macoma's (*Macoma secta*). Generally, at 2 inches long, the Bodega Tellin is smaller than the White Sand Macoma, and it has a narrow, oblong shell. It is a relatively rare find on Southern California beaches, due in part to its delicate shells, which snap very easily. At times, however, the shells occur in fair numbers on sandy beaches, such as Coronado State Beach in San Diego County.

Top: *California Jackknife* (Tagelus californianus) Middle: *Purplish Tagelus* (Tagelus divisus) Bottom: *Rosy Jackknife* (Solen rostriformis)

Bodega Tellin (Tellina bodegensis)

Pismo Clam (*Tivela stultorum*)

The shells of full-grown Pismo Clams (*Tivela stultorum*), up to 6 inches long, are so chunky and shiny that people mistake them for fragments of glazed ceramic. Pismo Clams range in color from glossy tan to dark brown, and some have brown stripes on a tan shell.

At one time this clam's future was endangered because people harvested it heavily for its tasty meat. Now the California Department of Fish and Game regulates harvesting levels for all shellfish, so hopefully the Pismo Clam's numbers will never be as low as they once were.

The Pismo Clam's life cycle is representative of most clams. The adult female releases millions of extremely tiny eggs during each spawning period. Within a day or so of fertilization the egg develops into a free-swimming larva called a *veliger,* and within weeks it resembles a tiny version of an adult. At this stage it develops byssal threads—thin, strong strings of protein the clam produces from its mantle. It wraps these threads around grains of sand, anchoring itself to the ocean floor in shallow water. These thin strands keep it from being swept into deeper water where it would perish. Imagine being so small that a few grains of sand would be enough to anchor you to the earth!

The young clam clings to sand particles until it is big enough and heavy enough to burrow. An adult Pismo, like other clams in the Venus family, relies on its weight and its muscular foot to remain under the sand. From the safety of its burrow, it extends a siphon to feed on microscopic algae, bacteria, the spawn of other creatures, and small decaying bits of plant and animal matter that float past in the water.

Pismo Clam (Tivela stultorum)

Different patterns and shades of Pismo Clams

Pacific Butter Clam (*Saxidomus nuttalli*)
Pacific White Venus (*Amiantis callosa*)

Most clams of the Venus family have thick, round white shells, but picking the exact species can be tricky even for experts. To identify a shell, they examine hinge type, internal muscle attachment, and tissue parts—most or all of which may have disappeared by the time a shell is washed ashore. If sand and water haven't eroded the outside sculpting, you can examine this to determine what species from the Venus family you have found. Look for rough bands on the exterior of the 5-inch-long Pacific Butter Clam (*Saxidomus nuttalli*), and a pink or purple rim along the interior. The 4-inch-long Pacific White Venus (*Amiantis callosa*) has a glossier shell and nearly perfect concentric bands. Neither species has crosshatching rays.

The body structure of a clam leaves tracks on the inside surface of a shell. Clamshells have two small, oblong or disk-shaped scars with a thin line running between them. The size, shape, and placement of these scars indicate where the clam's adductor muscle was attached. This is the strong muscle the clam uses to pull its shell closed and keep it shut, protecting itself from all but the most-determined predators.

The thin line that runs from one adductor scar to the other is where the mantle was attached; it's called the *pallial line.* The incurving sweep in the line is called the *pallial sinus,* and this is where the muscles that retracted the animal's siphon were attached. For Pacific Butter Clams, the pallial sinus is C shaped, and for the Pacific White Venus, it is Z shaped.

Pacific Butter Clam (Saxidomus nuttalli)

Pacific White Venus (Amiantis callosa)

Wavy Venus (*Chione undatella*)
California Venus (*Chione californiensis*)
Smooth Venus (*Chione fluctifraga*)

People like the taste of clams, but locally they may not be the best food choice. A great deal of the Southern California shoreline is urbanized, and some towns have street runoff that is channeled into the ocean, polluting the inshore waters—not the ideal environment for a food source. There are also red tides, which are caused by an overgrowth of microscopic ocean organisms. Because all clams are filter feeders, they consume large amounts of these natural organisms, which build up in their systems and can be toxic to humans and other mammals that feed on them (see *Red Tides,* page 144). Check fishing regulations (California Department of Fish and Game) for catch limits and safe times of the year for clamming.

Chione species have chunky, chalky shells that are 2½ inches long and can be difficult to tell apart. All of them are adapted to the sandy and muddy bottoms of sheltered beaches and coastal wetlands where they burrow just a few inches below the surface. If you look closely you can see the subtle differences between each species. The Wavy Venus (*Chione undatella*) is the fattest of the three, the tallest, and the most globular, and it has a grid pattern of rays and bands that are evenly spaced. The California Venus (*Chione californiensis*) has a few raised concentric bands that overlay thin, nearly flat rays. The Smooth Venus (*Chione fluctifraga*) looks very much like a Wavy Venus, but it has a larger grid pattern that looks like erosion has worn it smooth. The grid of bands and rays gives these clams traction so they can grip a slick substrate of mud and sand. Researchers haven't figured out why there are three virtually identical, yet distinct, *Chione* species in Southern California, but the subtle differences in the grid patterns of their shells illustrate the amazing variety of marine life!

Left: *Wavy Venus* (Chione undatella) Middle: *California Venus* (Chione californiensis)
Right: *Smooth Venus* (Chione fluctifraga)

Rough-Sided Littleneck (*Prototkaca laciniata*)
Pacific Littleneck (*Prototkaca staminea*)

It can be tricky identifying whether you have the shell of a Rough-Sided Littleneck (*Protothaca laciniata*) or a Wavy Venus (*Chione undatella*) from the outside of the shell. You have to look inside the shell and trace the pallial line if possible. The Rough-Sided Littleneck's line is Z shaped, while the Wavy Venus's is shaped like a bow and follows the curve of the shell without a discernable pallial sinus. The outer surface of the Pacific Littleneck (*Protothaca staminea*) has fainter crosshatching than the Rough-Sided Littleneck. Because of this faint crosshatching, it resembles a cockle shell, and one of its common names is *Rock Cockle*. Some Pacific Littlenecks are solid beige, but others have brown zigzags decorating their round, 2- to 3-inch, cream-colored shells.

The astronomical odds against the survival of a Pacific Little-neck, or any clam, are bewildering. When clams spawn, they simply broadcast eggs and sperm into the ocean, which depend on currents to bring them together for fertilization. The spawn becomes part of the plankton, floating in the water with no protection against the thousands, if not millions of creatures that depend on it as food. If a fertilized egg hatches, the baby, or *veliger,* must survive long enough to grow a protective shell and nestle into the ocean bottom—in the correct environment to which its species is adapted.

Initially the veliger weighs very little, so even after it reaches this stage it is at the mercy of tides and predators. Slowly, molecule by molecule, it builds a shell. Over the years, it breeds and grows in its habitat, filtering debris out of the water as it hides from predators and withstands changing ocean temperatures and currents. Then when it dies, its shell becomes a part of the sediment that provides an anchor and hiding place for other animals. If left undisturbed for a long time in fine sediments, shells may become fossilized in sedimentary rocks. Often, however, a shell is washed onto the beach where people pick it up and seldom consider the astounding life cycle that the creature has completed.

*Comparison of Rough-Sided Littleneck (Protothaca laciniata) and Wavy Venus (Chione undatella).
The littleneck is on the left in each photo and the Wavy Venus is on the right.*

Pacific Littleneck (Protothaca staminea)

*Shale with
mollusk fossils*

Nuttall's Cockle (*Clinocardium nuttallii*)
Pacific Eggcockle (*Laevicardium substriatum*)
Pacific Cockle (*Trachycardium quadragenarium*)

In other places in the world, cockles are found along rocky coasts, but the cockles along Southern California shores are unique; they have adapted to sandy habitats. They have very short siphons, so they live only a few inches below the sand's surface where currents, tides, and shifting sand affect them. Each member of the cockle family, though, has an unusually large foot, which it uses to hop out of the sand—a startling sight! Their mobility is a real asset. It allows them to shift their positions to adjust to changes in their environment.

At first glance, Nuttall's Cockles (*Clinocardium nuttallii*) look similar to some species of Venus clams. Like Pacific Littlenecks (*Protothaca staminea*), they have thin rays on the outside of their shells; however, cockle shells are more spherical. In fact, *cardium,* an element of their scientific names, is Latin for "heart." It refers to the cockle's valentine-shaped profile when the two shells are clamped together. Unlike many bivalves, such as the White Sand Macoma (*Macoma secta*), the two halves are symmetrical. Cockles also form uniform humps on both shells, which are indicative of the symmetrical structure of their internal organs.

A Nuttall's Cockle has rays that are more pronounced than those of the Pacific Eggcockle (*Laevicardium substriatum*), which has minute, fine-lined rays that are barely noticeable. Both clams are tan and mottled with slightly darker blotches, but the Nuttall's shells are heavier, darker, and much larger (up to 4 inches as opposed to the 1-inch Pacific Eggcockle). The Pacific Cockle (*Trachycardium quadragenarium*) is about 5 inches long when full grown, and it is the largest cockle in Southern California. It has small bumps or spines near the edge of its shell, though these may have been worn smooth if the shell is older or the cockle lived in an area with coarse sand.

Nuttall's Cockles
(Clinocardium
nuttallii)

Pacific Eggcockles
(Laevicardium
substriatum)

Pacific Cockle
(Trachycardium
quadragenarium)

Pacific Gaper (*Tresus nuttallii*)
Hemphill's Surfclam (*Mactromeris hemphillii*)

The Pacific Gaper (*Tresus nuttallii*) is one of the largest clams on Southern California beaches, growing up to 8 inches long. It has thick, chalky shells with concentric growth bands, which cause it to look similar to the Pacific Butter Clam (*Saxidomus nuttalli*), and they both have C-shaped pallial sinuses. However, you can instantly identify gapers even if their shells are badly eroded because they have distinctive bowl-shaped hinges. The gaper is named for the *gape,* or gap, between its shells, from which the clam extends its large, fleshy siphon.

Smaller gapers, like the Hemphill's Surfclam (*Mactromeris hemphillii*), have smooth, thin shells, though they still have bowl-shaped hinges. Hemphill's Surfclams and young Pacific Gapers live fairly close to the surface of the sand and have the ability to reburrow if they are disturbed. However, the adult Pacific Gaper depends on the safety of a deep and undisturbed burrow. Because its foot does not keep up with the growth of its shell and siphon, the Pacific Gaper cannot reburrow if it is dug up. It lives way below the surface where it is protected from all but the largest predators, such as rays. From the comfort of its burrow, it extends its siphon to the water, which can be an amazing 3 feet above the clam. Only the tip of the siphon peeks above the surface of the sand, and you may see it at extreme low tides.

Siphons have two purposes: to suck in water containing plankton and decaying bits of plant and animal matter, which the clam filters through its gills into its stomach; and to expel wastes. Occasionally, at low tide, you can locate large gapers when they spurt water several feet in the air. No one knows why they do this; perhaps they are clearing their siphons of excess water and debris.

Pacific Gaper (Tresus nuttallii)

Hemphill's Surfclam (Mactromeris hemphillii)

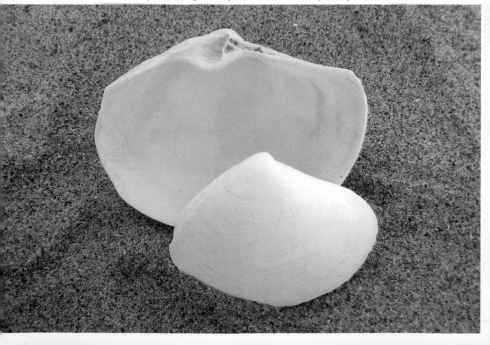

Pandora (*Pandora punctata*)
Ribbed Mussel (*Geukensia demissa*)

Occasionally beachcombers may find the beautiful and distinctive Pandora (*Pandora punctata*). This clam lives in the subtidal zone, the threshold to the deeper sea. At first glance, it may be mistaken for a fragment of weathered shell, such as that of a mussel, but the Pandora has a unique crescent shape, and the upper edge of its shell folds inward.

This lovely little 1- to 1½-inch-long shell is iridescent mother-of-pearl both inside and out. Interestingly, color pigments do not produce iridescence; it is the effect produced when light reflects off the layers of a shell. All mollusk shells are made of the same material, crystals of calcium carbonate, but each species's differing internal chemistry affects how the crystals and layers develop. The patterns of these layers determine the level of the shell's iridescence, glossiness, or chalkiness, and its strength as well. Think of the layers as strips of papier-mâché: on its own, an individual strip is not very strong; when combined with interlocking and overlapping strips, however, it helps create a strong structure. Many people seem to feel that things we cannot see are somehow inherently unattractive; and they are amazed by how lovely some of these creatures that spend their lives hidden away, like the Pandora, can be.

Mussel shells are common on Southern California beaches, and for ten thousand years or more coastal Indians used them as food and tools. The 5-inch-long Ribbed Mussel (*Geukensia demissa*), however, is a foreign invader that was introduced into California waters from the East Coast in the late nineteenth century, probably carried to the Pacific in the ballast of a sailing ship. Whether it filled an ecologically "empty" position or pushed out native creatures, the Ribbed Mussel has adapted well to the Pacific. While indigenous mussels such as the California Mussel (*Mytilus californianus*) and Bay Mussel (*Mytilus* species) are rock dwellers (see the Rocky Shores chapter), the Ribbed Mussel lives on sand, and hundreds of them can be found sitting on the muddy bottoms of salt marshes and shallow, quiet bays. They filter debris from the water, and are food for some coastal birds.

You can easily identify mussels by their distinctive shape: they are roughly oval, pinched at one end, slightly flattened at the other, with a hump like the back of a serving spoon. The exterior of a mussel's shell is dark blue or black, but over time the outer layers wear away, exposing white mother-of-pearl. Ribbed Mussel shells are narrower than other mussel species, and they are striped with a series of ridges. They are more delicate than other mussel shells, perhaps because Ribbed Mussels live in quiet waters and do not need to develop thick shells to withstand beating waves.

Pandora
(Pandora
punctata)

Ribbed Mussels
(Geukensia
demissa)

Pearly Jingle (*Anomia peruviana*)

Fragile Pearly Jingle shells (*Anomia peruviana*) gleam on the shore like 2- to 3-inch disks of silver, gold, orange, white, or black. These soft, lustrous shells easily crumble to a fine talc-like powder, adding glitter to the golden sands of Southern California. The jingle shell is more fragile than many other bivalve shells, but it is made of the same material, calcium carbonate, which is secreted by the mantle, a thin fleshy part of a mollusk's body. Although each species of mollusk has a set body and shell plan, each individual creature is as unique as a snowflake or fingerprint. This is especially noticeable with Pearly Jingles, because there is great variation in the shape and color of their shells.

Pearly Jingles do not burrow into sand. They are *epifaunal,* meaning they attach to rocks, shells, and each other in the subtidal zone. Each jingle secretes byssal threads—thin strands of protein that look something like brown or golden strings of seaweed—that anchor the jingle to its substrate. The threads emerge from a hole near the hinge of the bottom valve, which is horseshoe shaped. Some people notice the Pearly Jingle's horseshoe-shaped shell when they are beachcombing, but assume that it is a broken piece of shell; however, it is actually a special beachcombing find. Most of these shells remain firmly attached to their substrate after the Pearly Jingles have perished, and seldom wash ashore.

Although they live on a rocky substrate, Pearly Jingles are more commonly found on sandy beaches. Because onshore and offshore terrain can be very different, the presence of a sandy beach does not mean that rocky jingle habitat isn't nearby. If subtidal rocks extend onto a beach, though, then rocky shores result, and Pearly Jingle shells are usually smashed to pieces before they reach the shore. Where subtidal rocks give way to sandy beaches, however, jingle shells are common beachcombing finds.

Pearly Jingle (Anomia peruviana)

A Pearly Jingle's horseshoe-shaped bottom valve

FREE-SWIMMING BIVALVES (SCALLOPS)

Unlike sand-dwelling bivalves, free-swimming mollusks do not burrow. They "swim" by clapping their shells as though they are taking bites out of the water. Like all bivalves, these free swimmers feed through a siphon, filtering microorganisms, bacteria, and decaying plant and animal matter from the ocean.

Pacific Calico Scallop (*Argopecten ventricosus*)
Reddish Scallop (*Chlamys rubida*)

Pacific Calico Scallops (*Argopecten ventricosus*) and Reddish Scallops (*Chlamys rubida*) are the gypsies of the bivalve world—no settled life for them hidden in a sandy burrow or attached to a rock! They spend their lives swimming freely in the subtidal zone along bays with sandy bottoms. More complex than most bivalves, scallops have tentacles that protrude from their shells and help them sense danger. When they do sense danger, they escape by snapping their shells open and shut, "flying" through the water. Scallop bodies are also rimmed with tiny gleaming balls that are actually light-gathering eyes. This seems odd because scallops do not have heads, but then no bivalves do.

The Reddish Scallop is very small—1 inch long at most—and has flat, smooth rays that may be any shade from yellow to orangish red. The 4-inch-long Pacific Calico Scallop has deeply grooved rays and a cream-colored shell that is mottled red or orange, but some are almost black, though the red and orange markings remain faintly visible under the sooty color. The black coloring is caused by the creature's diet—too much organic material like dirt, mud, or tar. This organic material can occur naturally because of erosion or the geology of underwater terrain, or it can be a product of pollution.

Pacific Calico Scallop (Argopecten ventricosus)

Reddish Scallop (Chlamys rubida)

Rock Scallop (*Hinnites giganteus*)
Kelpweed Scallop (*Leptopecten latiauratus*)
Hemphill's Lima (*Lima hemphilli*)

The Rock Scallop (*Hinnites giganteus*) starts life as a free-swimming gypsy, but once it matures it attaches to a rock with byssal threads and like an oyster grows crusty, irregular layers, making the shell up to 8 inches long. It retains its telltale scallop shape above the hinge: a fan of grooved rays.

The 2-inch-long Kelpweed Scallop (*Leptopecten latiauratus*) has a similar life cycle, but as its name implies, it attaches to kelp. It has little bumps or knuckles along its rays. Hemphill's Lima (*Lima hemphilli*) is a 1-inch-long bivalve that nestles among rocks and debris. Like a scallop, it has eyes, and it can swim to escape would-be predators or to find a different food source. It is often called *File Clam* because its shell is white like most clams, and its thin rays look as if they have been filed or etched onto the delicate shell.

Rock Scallop
(Hinnites
giganteus)

Kelpweed Scallop
(Leptopecten
latiauratus)

Hemphill's Lima
(Lima hemphilli)

GASTROPODS (SNAILS)

Also known as *univalves* and *marine snails,* gastropods are single-shelled mollusks. The body plan of most gastropods is more complex than bivalves. Gastropods have a head with sensory organs—eyes and antennae. They may move slowly, but they are more mobile than bivalves, creeping along on their "stomach-foot" (*gastro* is Greek for "stomach," and *poda* is Greek for "foot") searching for food. Many marine snails eat marine vegetation, algae, which they scrape off rocks with a tiny tongue called a *radula,* which contains minute but hard teeth. Some gastropods are carnivores, though, drilling into other mollusks with their radula. Although marine snails have more variation to their shells, they are very similar to their land relative the garden snail.

California Horn Snail (*Cerithidea californica*)

Because of their diet, most gastropods live along rocky shores; however, there are a hardy few that have adapted to sandy or muddy substrates. The California Horn Snail (*Cerithidea californica*) is the most common and visible gastropod along muddy bays, salt marshes, shallow-water lagoons, and mudflats. At low tide you may see hundreds scavenging for bits of plant or animal debris along the bottom of small pools. You may also see them lying on their sides on the shore as though they are playing dead, waiting for the incoming water, which protects them from predators and keeps them from drying out.

The California Horn Snail is an important source of food for fish and some shorebirds. Superficially, it is similar to the spindle-shaped Wentletrap (*Opalia* species) that lives and dines on anemones, but the California Horn Snail is larger (about 1 inch long), and depending on its environment, its shell color ranges from off-white to red or dark brown. Horn snails with reddish brown shades occur where the substrate is mostly sand. Many of the horn snail shells found in coastal wetlands are chalky white and very fragile. Researchers believe that the salinity level and lack of wave action in these wetlands may have something to do with this. You may notice large numbers of black horn snails in very muddy and polluted wetlands. Their dark color could be the result of natural color variations or pollution, or they could be a subspecies adapted to environments with more organic debris. The California Horn Snail is related to the odd Scaly Tube Snail (*Serpulorbis squamigerus*).

California Horn Snail (Cerithidea californica)

Lewis's Moonsnail (*Lunatia lewisi* or *Euspira lewisii*)
Recluz's Moonsnail (*Neverita reclusiana*)

A moonsnail hunts in the subtidal zone, skulking along on its stomach-foot as it searches for sand dwellers to sup upon. Moonsnails are as round as the full moon and shaped much like garden snails, but they have heavier, thicker shells. Once a moonsnail spots its prey, it is relentless. Since a clam's defense is to clamp its valves shut, a moonsnail does not waste its time trying to pull the shells apart. Instead it drills a round, beveled hole through the shell with its radula, and then dines on the clam's muscle. Moonsnails also prey on each other, and the younger, smaller snails are often the victims. When a moonsnail dies, the Moon Snail Hermit Crab (*Isocheles pilosus*) may move into the shell it leaves behind.

The Lewis's Moonsnail (*Lunatia lewisi* or *Euspira lewisii*) is the largest gastropod living in the sandy intertidal zone. The shell of an adult can be up to 5 inches across; when living, its huge foot can extend another 4 to 5 inches around it. It also has a thick, slimy mantle that covers most of its shell to protect it from abrading sand. Though the Recluz's Moonsnail (*Neverita reclusiana*), with a maximum diameter of 3 inches, is a little smaller than the Lewis's, both are tan and brown and look very similar. To distinguish the two species you need to examine the umbilicus, which is on the underside of the snail's shell near its aperture. If there is a hole shaped like a belly button next to the aperture, it is a Lewis's Moonsnail; it is a Recluz's Moonsnail if the area is smooth.

Lewis's Moonsnail (Lunatia lewisi *or* Euspira lewisii)

Recluz's Moonsnail (Neverita reclusiana)

Spiral Moonsnail (*Neverita helicoides*)
Western Baby's Ear (*Sinum scopulosum*)

The 3-inch-long Spiral Moonsnail (*Neverita helicoides*) is flatter than the other two moonsnails, and it has gray and brown lines on its cream-colored shell. This species seems to have migrated from Baja California, Mexico, and can be found as far north as Los Angeles County. Western Baby's Ear (*Sinum scopulosum*) is an unmistakable snail: it has a nearly flat, 1-inch shell with a wide opening, and it is white or cream colored with a glossy interior.

You may think you've spotted a complete moonsnail shell when you see its characteristic "eye" (the central swirl) peering up at you from the sand, only to discover that it's a fragment. Bat Rays (*Myliobatus californicus*) and small sand-dwelling sharks eat moonsnails. They crunch through the tough shells and leave the broken pieces to wash ashore.

Some beachcombing discoveries are really surprising. Moonsnail egg-casings, also called *sand collars,* appear on the beach during summer. To create a sand collar, a female secretes mucus from her mantle, which she then molds with her foot and binds with sand. She lays eggs against the inner wall of the collar, and sandwiches the eggs with another protective layer of sand and mucus. The eggs are so tiny that the collar looks like one thin but solid layer to us. The young go through several stages of development until they hatch, crawling out of the collar as tiny but perfect versions of adult moonsnails. A sand collar from a Lewis's Moonsnail is 3 to 5 inches wide. Although it resembles the top of a dirty liter-sized bottle, it's a fascinating piece of nature. There's no point in collecting a sand collar, though, since it doesn't last for long. When the casing dries, it crumbles back to sand.

Spiral Moonsnail (Neverita helicoides)

Western Baby's Ear (Sinum scopulosum)

Moonsnail sand collar

Moonsnail victims

Echinoderms

SAND DOLLAR

Sand Dollar (*Dendraster excentricus*)

The Sand Dollar (*Dendraster excentricus*), shaped like an old-fashioned silver dollar, is a treasure of a find for most beachcombers. Many people don't know that when it's alive, this intriguing creature has a purple disk, also called a *test,* and short purple spines. It is only after it dies that, little by little, the spines rub off and the disk bleaches from purple to gray to silvery white.

Sand Dollars reproduce by releasing sex cells into the water. The larvae are free-swimming for a time, then they settle to the ocean bottom when their tests begin to grow. Like its relatives—urchins and sea stars—the Sand Dollar has tiny tube feet that help it maneuver. Plowing its rim into the sand, the Sand Dollar wriggles its feet and spines to achieve a vertical or semivertical position. They stand on their rims in rows under the waves in the subtidal zone, and crowd together in amazing numbers. In fact, there can be over five hundred Sand Dollars per square yard of ocean floor.

Sand acts as ballast, keeping the creature anchored to the ocean floor, while its tube feet and spines work together capturing organic debris, plankton, and tiny fish. The spines are covered with tiny hair-like cilia that make live Sand Dollars almost fuzzy to the touch. The cilia move food into the Sand Dollar's mouth—the round hole located on the underside of its shell. Around the mouth, strong muscles work bony plates in a specialized jaw called *Aristotle's lantern.* Sand Dollars are very effective hunters.

You won't find Sand Dollar tests on every beach. Their presence is a clue to offshore terrain, which has to be level and sandy to support a colony of Sand Dollars. The beach itself must be flat or have a gradual slope, too; if it is too steep, the tests of these interesting animals do not wash ashore in one piece.

Sand Dollars (Dendraster excentricus)

Arthropods

CRABS

Moon Snail Hermit Crab (*Isocheles pilosus*)

If you spot an improbably fast moonsnail scurrying along the sand, look closely—it's probably a Moon Snail Hermit Crab (*Isocheles pilosus*). These crustaceans move into empty moonsnail shells and live in offshore waters. They burrow in soft, wet sand to escape predators like rays and small sharks. Moon Snail Hermit Crabs are yellowish white, have tiny hairlike prickles, and can be quite large—some live in shells that are 3 to 4 inches across.

Although they have hard, jointed legs, a hermit crab does not have a hard exoskeleton covering its entire body like lobsters and true crabs. A hermit crab has a soft belly that it protects by living in a cast-off gastropod shell. It coils its tail in a shell and clings to the shell's inner whorls. Predators have a difficult time dislodging an entrenched hermit crab. Each hermit crab species has adapted to a particular shape of shell, and there are hermit crabs adapted to the gastropod shells found along rocky shores (see the Rocky Shores chapter).

Moon Snail Hermit Crabs survive best in round, moonsnail shells, but if they cannot find ones large enough they move into whatever they can find. In areas where pollution has reduced biodiversity, they may try to survive in cups, bottles, and other garbage that litters the bottom of some bays.

Moon Snail Hermit Crab (Isocheles pilosus)

Pacific Sand Crab (*Emerita analoga*)
Spiny Sand Crab (*Blepharipoda occidentalis*)

At the water's edge, look for an air hole in the sand about as big around as a drinking straw. If you dig quickly into the soft sand you might find a handful of pink and gray Pacific Sand Crabs (*Emerita analoga*) that are less than 1 inch long. Also known as the *Mole Crab,* this crab has jointed and hinged legs like all crustaceans, but its legs occur directly under its body rather than extending out to the side. This adaptation enables it to live beneath the sand. If you hold a Pacific Sand Crab in your hand, it will kick its legs as it tries to burrow to safety. The Pacific Sand Crab can quickly vanish in wet sand. Although it looks as if its digging head-first, it actually backs into the sand.

There is a triangular armored flap called a *telson* on the underside of most crab species. To identify a Pacific Sand Crab's gender, gently lift the flap and look for three sets of hairlike legs called *pleopods*. Males don't have them, but females use them to hold their eggs in place. An egg-carrying female will have a bright orange cluster of eggs. She carries them with her until they hatch, though if stressed she may eat them. In midsummer, occasionally the tide line is awash with what looks like living, mobile grains of rice. These are baby sand crabs. They are an important food source for birds and fish.

The larger, 3-inch-long Spiny Sand Crab (*Blepharipoda occidentalis*) is pale gray and has fierce-looking protective spines along its legs and carapace (the upper shell of its exoskeleton). It lives in the deeper sub-tidal zone, so people rarely find one alive on the beach. However, its cast-off carapace commonly washes ashore when the Spiny Sand Crab grows and sheds its outer coverings.

Both the Pacific Sand Crab and Spiny Sand Crab have three pairs of antennae that allow them to survive under the sand. The first pair forms a tube that siphons water from above the sand. The second pair filters food from the water. And the third pair keeps sand out of the crab's mouth. Complex but efficient!

Pacific Sand Crab (Emerita analoga)

Pacific Sand Crab with eggs

Spiny Sand Crab (Blepharipoda occidentalis)

Cnidarians

HYDROIDS

Clam Hydroid (*Clytia bakeri*)
Plume Hydroid (*Aglaophenia* species)
Turgid Hydroid (*Sertularella* species)

At the surf line, you may notice that some bean clams sport "beards" that look like tiny clumps of golden seaweed or byssal threads. Those clumps are actually Clam Hydroids (*Clytia bakeri*), animals that attach themselves to the edges of shallow-water, surf-dwelling clams. Each clump of hydroids is actually a colony of tiny individuals called *polyps*. From their perch at the end of a clam, polyps extend into the water above the sand to feed on microorganisms. Nutrients are shared among the colony via the stalk. Other polyps are specialized for defensive or reproductive purposes only. Every few years there is a population explosion of these creatures, and almost all the bean clams along Southern California beaches have hydroids on them. In other years they are extremely rare.

Marine biologists know very little about the relationship between Clam Hydroids and clams. Researchers are trying to determine if the creatures somehow benefit each other, and they have several hypotheses. It's possible that hydroids filter particles that might cause infections in clams. Perhaps the clam merely provides a safe platform for the hydroid. Researchers also have theories about the hydroid's boom-and-bust life cycle. They think it's possible that the two animals compete for food, and after the hydroids have reached a level of overgrowth, they die back. Or perhaps the Clam Hydroid disappears because of periodic changes in the weather and water temperature. For now, the relationship between the two species is just one of the interesting mysteries of beach wildlife.

Other hydroids, such as the beautiful Plume Hydroid (*Aglaophenia* species), attach to mussel shells along rocks and pilings, or they entwine themselves in kelp. The Turgid Hydroid (*Sertularella* species) looks very much like miniature yellow zigzags or lightning bolts attached to kelp, rocks, and pilings.

Clam Hydroid (Clytia bakeri) *on a bean clam*

Hydroids (Clytia *species*) *on mussels*

Plume Hydroid
(Aglaophenia *species*)

Turgid Hydroid
(Sertularella *species*)

Mini Habitat

BROWN ALGAE OR KELP

The term *seaweed* commonly refers to marine plants as well as algae. Algae are nonvascular members of the plant kingdom that are found wherever there is water and sunshine. Species sizes range from microscopic single-celled dinoflagellates and diatoms to 100-foot-long strands of kelp. Algal species are placed in divisions based on their colors, and along the beaches and shores of Southern California you may notice pink, green, or brown species. The brown species are commonly called *kelp*. All algae are important to the marine environment, and through the expiration of oxygen, vital to the health of the planet.

Giant Kelp (*Macrocystis pyrifera*)

Giant Kelp (*Macrocystis pyrifera*), which grows just offshore like a towering underwater forest, is Southern California's most important seaweed. Not only is it essential oceanic habitat for many species, it is also utilized by humans. Kelp is harvested at the surface of the ocean and used in hundreds of products, including cosmetics and food. Since it can grow up to 2 feet a day, the removal of the top fronds allows sun to reach lower layers, stimulating growth. Proper harvesting can actually benefit wildlife.

On the other hand, warm water can destroy kelp. As part of the El Niño weather pattern, every seven years or so warm water from the southern hemisphere migrates north. This causes extreme weather patterns and above-average warming of Southern California waters, both of which can wipe out large sections of kelp forest. Fortunately, kelp grows fast and can recover quickly after an El Niño has passed. Dredging and pollution are another matter, and both have stressed Southern California's environment. There are areas of the California Bight that still don't have the lush kelp forests that once thrived.

Choppy seas caused by a change in ocean currents or heavy swells from bad weather uproot pieces of kelp. High tides carry some of them to shore, where they remain stranded until the next tide carries them out. A pile of seaweed is called a *wrack* (meaning "driven" or "destroyed by the sea"). On level sandy beaches, beach tractors often remove wracks for aesthetic reasons. This is a shame, because wracks contribute to a richer ecosystem, supporting native scavengers like birds, sand flies, and small crustaceans.

The tops of underwater kelp forests are visible on the surface of the ocean.

Giant Kelp (Macrocystis pyrifera) *wracks*

PARTS OF KELP

Kelp serves many functions within the marine ecosystem: food, shelter, an attaching surface, and hunting grounds for predators. This makes a wrack very rewarding to explore—a place to find snail, fish, and shark eggs, as well as a host of bizarre creatures. You have to find a freshly washed-up wrack, though, because gulls quickly pick them over, and even land creatures such as ladybugs scavenge wracks for meals.

The broad leaflike parts of kelp are the *fronds* or *blades,* the ropy stem is called the *stipe,* and the pointed bulbs are named *floats.* If you squeeze a float, it will explode with a little "pop," releasing gas. The floats keep kelp vertical in the water, so it can grow upright like a tree, toward the sun. The height to which Giant Kelp will grow is limited by the depth that sunlight penetrates the ocean—about 100 feet. Like most plants, it creates food through photosynthesis, and it needs sunlight in order to convert carbon dioxide and water molecules into the carbohydrates that provide it nutrients.

On the end of the stipe is a *holdfast.* As its name implies, the holdfast's function is to hold *fast* (the English expression for "tightly") to the bottom of the ocean. This thick, bulbous clump looks a bit like a root, but unlike a land plant the tendrils of the holdfast do not absorb nutrients. Their sole purpose is to anchor kelp to rocks and crevices offshore. Kelp cannot grow on a smooth, sandy ocean floor, so even if a wrack occurs on a sandy beach, the ocean bottom offshore must be rocky.

Fronds and stipe

Float

Holdfast

WILDLIFE ON KELP

Norris Top Snail (*Norrisia norrisi*)
Kelp Limpet (*Discurria insessa*)

Talk about being eaten out of house and home! Some animals eat the kelp they live on. The Norris Top Snail (*Norrisia norrisi*) munches its way through the fronds and stipe of its neighborhood. You often can find its shell or shell fragments entangled in a wrack. The Norris Top Snail has a 2-inch-wide, round, brown shell that resembles a moonsnail's shell, only flatter, and a body that is fringed with red color.

The Kelp Limpet (*Discurria insessa*), another single-shelled mollusk, is also a voracious eater. It likes to feed on Feather Boa Kelp (*Egregia* species), a brown seaweed that grows in the intertidal zone. Feather Boa Kelp has short, feathery blades along its stipes—making it look a bit like a feather boa. Limpets dig into both stipes and blades as they feed on Feather Boa Kelp and leave home scar depressions and other tracks. Home scar depressions are indentations with raised edges and they are where a limpet rests when it isn't eating. There are two types of limpet track that I have observed. One is a hole in kelp where a limpet has eaten all the way through a stipe or blade; the other is a groove, where a limpet has grazed for a while and then moved on. Unlike home scar depressions, grooves do not have raised edges.

Some researchers theorize that limpet-damaged kelp is less prone to being uprooted in severe storms because it has fewer and lighter fronds to be entangled in the surf. More research is needed, though, because both limpet-damaged and undamaged wracks of kelp wash up on Southern California beaches.

Norris Top Snail (Norrisia norrisi)

Kelp Limpet (Discurria insessa)　　　　*Feather Boa Kelp* (Egregia *species*)

Scaly Tube Snail (*Serpulorbis squamigerus*)
Shield-Back Kelp Crab (*Pugettia producta*)

Other creatures, such as the Kelpweed Scallop (*Leptopecten latiauratus*), Scaly Tube Snail (*Serpulorbis squamigerus*), and Shield-Back Kelp Crab (*Pugettia producta*) use kelp as a pier from which to fish. Scaly Tube Snails may gather in the tangle of a holdfast where they build 3- to 5-inch-long, tube-shaped shells that coil and twist around each other in weird, abstract designs. Each ½-inch opening in a cluster houses a separate snail. Since this snail's shell is cemented to its substrate, it has a unique way of capturing its food: it casts a net of mucus into the water to ensnare passing organic debris, which it then draws back into its shell to eat. These strange creatures are often confused with tube-building marine snails, but they are univalve mollusks and are related to the California Horn Snail (*Cerithidea californica*).

The Shield-Back Kelp Crab eats kelp and lives its entire life in the kelp habitat, signaling to potential rivals and mating among the fronds. During winter months its diet changes; it stalks along kelp preying on hydroids and bryozoans. Its shield-shaped carapace is about 3 inches across, but with its long legs sticking out to each side, this crab can be an intimidating 8 inches wide. Its glossy yellow to brown color keeps it well camouflaged.

*Scaly Tube Snails
(Serpulorbis
squamigerus),
in a kelp holdfast*

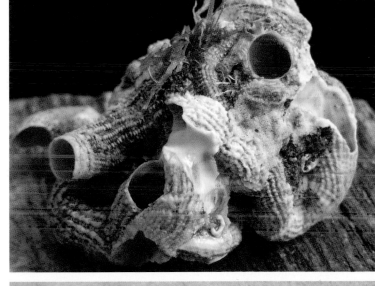

Scaly Tube Snails

*Shield-Back
Kelp Crab
(Pugettia
producta)*

Kelp Lace (*Membranipora membranacea*)
Frost-Spot Corambe (*Corambe pacifica*)
Kelp Isopod (*Idotea wosnesenskii*)

Sometimes mistaken for splotches of white sand or minute fish eggs, Kelp Lace (*Membranipora membranacea*) is a compound organism composed of individuals, also called *zooids*. Although it seems strange, a single creature can be made up of thousands of individuals. Each tiny dot is a zooid with a specialized job—eating, breeding, guarding, cleaning, or filling in spaces—within the colony. Colonies can encrust kelp in a beautiful fan pattern; other Kelp Lace colonies may cover a kelp float like a lacy sleeve. Kelp Lace's phylum Ectoprocta (also known as *bryozoans* or *moss animals*) contains over four thousand species. Some form twiglike colonies or balls of twigs, others form leaflike colonies, while others encrust rocks, shells, kelp, and other seaweeds.

If you find Kelp Lace, then the Frost-Spot Corambe (*Corambe pacifica*) is probably nearby. It is a gastropod—a sea slug or nudibranch—that lacks a shell. It preys exclusively on Kelp Lace, and because of its translucent body and tiny spots, it looks like a drop of water—an adaptation that camouflages it from predators. The Frost-Spot Corambe looks as if it would be soft and slimy, but actually it is firm to the touch and feels a bit like a jelly bean. It is a delicate creature though, and if you decide to touch it or any live creature please be gentle.

The Kelp Isopod (*Idotea wosnesenskii*) is a 2-inch-long, insectlike creature that also scavenges on floating beds of kelp and other seaweeds. Its yellowish green color camouflages it from predators, and has led to its other common name: *Olive-Green Isopod*. Although it looks like a peculiar cross between a pill bug and a grasshopper, it is an arthropod, a phylum that includes crabs.

If you stumble upon a wrack on a sandy beach, take a moment to explore. It is just one of many small and fascinating habitats within the larger beach environment.

Kelp Lace covering a kelp float

Kelp Lace (Membranipora membranacea)

Frost-Spot Corambe

corambe eggs

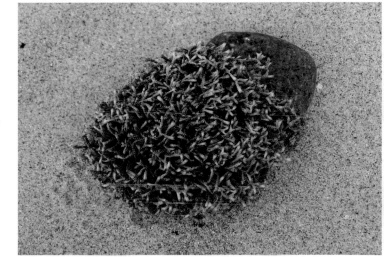

Bryozoan

Frost-Spot Corambe (Corambe pacifica)

Kelp Isopod (Idotea wosnesenskii)

Rocky Shores

Rocky shores occur at the foot of coastal bluffs and where the beach has eroded, leaving outcroppings along the coast of Southern California. Marine animals live on the rocks underwater at high tide and take shelter in tidepools at low tide. Although the majority of Southern California's natural coastline is sandy, man-made breakwaters (piles of boulders that shelter the shore from high waves) also create tidepools for marine life. Pilings under wharves, docks, and piers also collect many of the attaching and rock-boring creatures that live in natural tidepools.

Whether natural or man-made, rocky shores are tough places to live. The drag and pull of the ocean against rocky shores creates a harsh environment, and only the most tenacious and adaptable wildlife can survive in a place that is dry at low tide and submerged at high tide—yet exploring tidepools at low tide is one of the most rewarding beach wildlife experiences. You can find thousands of creatures in, on, under, and among the rocks.

The viewing strategy for rocky shores is a little different from beachcombing on sandy beaches. Although it is tempting to rush from tidepool to tidepool, it's actually more productive to choose a spot and wait patiently. After a few moments, pools that seemed barren will bloom with life as creatures begin to grow accustomed to you and your senses become more attuned to them. Tidepools are merely portals into the deeper coastal waters. In fact, our nearshore waters contain many species, most of which we are completely unaware of as we wade, swim, and surf.

Tidepool at La Jolla near San Diego

Wildlife on pier pilings

Mollusks

ROCK-DWELLING BIVALVES (MUSSELS, OYSTERS, PIDDOCKS)

Bivalves along rocky shores typically attach to rock in order to survive. In fact, large mussel beds are often the first thing people notice in tide-pool areas. Different groups of bivalves have developed different ways of attaching to substrates. Most mussels use byssal threads, oysters extrude a cementlike substance, and piddocks bore holes into rock. Except for having a smaller foot or no foot at all, the anatomy of a rock-dwelling bivalve is much the same as that of its sand-dwelling relatives.

California Mussel (*Mytilus californianus*)
Bay Mussel (*Mytilus* species; previously *M. edulis*)
Fat Horse Mussel (*Modiolus capax*)

Mussels congregate in beds on rocky outcroppings, on pilings under wharves and piers, and along natural or man-made breakwaters. Some mussel beds can be miles long—as extensive as the local rocky substrate. Intertidal mussel beds are exciting places to explore because of the diversity of animals found there. They shelter creatures from the wind, sun, and sea, and ocean debris collects in mussel beds and provides food for scavengers like crabs, snails, and worms. The beds also provide protection for attaching creatures such as barnacles, limpets, and anemones, as well as a solid surface for the holdfasts of seaweeds. And sea stars and drill snails, which prey upon mussels, are sure to be lurking nearby.

Although mussels appear to be cemented to rocks, they actually anchor to their substrate and each other with entangling byssal threads (occasionally called *gull lines*). Mussels, and many other bivalves, extrude these tough strands of protein that look like thin strings of seaweed or plants of some kind. If a mussel's byssal threads break, it will likely perish because mussels cannot regrow the threads fast enough to reattach to a rock before waves sweep them away.

Mussels are edible, but California state law prohibits people from collecting or eating them from May through October. Mussels are filter feeders, and during these months poisonous microscopic algae may build up in their systems and make them extremely toxic. The poison cannot be cooked out of them; and while the toxin does not harm the mussel, it can sicken and kill the mammals—mostly seals and sea lions—that eat them.

The California Mussel (*Mytilus californianus*) is one of the most adaptable and prolific creatures of Southern California. It is instantly

A mussel bed. A band of hydroids separates California Mussels (Mytilus californianus) *on top* *from Bay Mussels (Mytilus species) on bottom.*

California Mussel

recognizable by its dark blue outer shells, and curved ridges along its length. Although this mussel's exterior is plain, the inner shells are iridescent blue and gray with swirls of pink or green. For thousands of years, coastal Indians used this animal for food and tools. It is still used today: people collect it for food at certain times of year, and modern-day anglers chisel handfuls of mussels off pilings and use the bright orange meat for fish bait. If you broke an empty mussel shell and looked at a cross section, you'd see that it is composed of thin sheets or layers. For millennia, people have separated the iridescent inner layers of the shells and fashioned them into mosaic jewelry and other decorative items.

Although California Mussels broadcast eggs and sperm into the water like other bivalves, they are probably one of the most prolific breeders on the Pacific coast. They have longer spawn cycles and produce more sex cells than other species. In addition, the California Mussel can grow 3 inches long in one year—a prodigious growth rate for a mollusk. A full-grown California Mussel can be 8 inches long, and the older it is the heavier and thicker its shell will be. Shells are usually covered with a thin black skin called a *periostracum* that is secreted by the mantle. The periostracum protects the shell from abrasion and discourages attaching creatures from completely covering the mussel. On other species of bivalves, the periostracum may be gray, yellow, or brown, but on a mussel it is dark brown or black and particularly noticeable. It curls and flakes off as the shell dries.

The Bay Mussel (*Mytilus* species, previously *M. edulis*) is smaller, 3 to 4 inches long at most, mostly smooth with few or no ridges, and uniformly bluish black. Bay Mussel is a generic name that people use for several *Mytilus* species that are difficult to tell apart. Turbulent waves can break mussels off their rocks and wash them to shore, so the smaller Bay Mussels anchor themselves in California Mussel beds, where they are protected from the full brunt of the tides. You can also find them in large numbers along dock pilings in marinas and other calm waters.

The Fat Horse Mussel (*Modiolus capax*) also hunkers down within the mussel community for protection, but it usually burrows into cracks and crevices in rocks or at their bases. The Fat Horse Mussel is a broad, sturdy bivalve that grows about 4 inches long. Its shell is covered with a brown, fuzzy periostracum that is commonly called its *beard*. Most mussels are blue, but under the somewhat unattractive beard of the Fat Horse Mussel there is a layer of orange-colored shell, and the interior of this shell is an iridescent peach color.

Bay Mussels (Mytilus *species*)

*Interior of a
Fat Horse Mussel*

Fat Horse Mussel (Modiolus capax)

Agate Jewel Box (*Chama arcana*)
Pacific Oyster (*Crassostrea gigas*)
American Oyster (*Crassostrea virginica*)
California Oyster (*Ostrea lurida*)

If you see what looks like a piece of quartz along the rocky shoreline, look closely—it might be an Agate Jewel Box (*Chama arcana*). Rather than using byssal threads, this 2-inch-wide bivalve secretes glue and cements itself to rocks. Sometimes dozens and even hundreds of Agate Jewel Boxes congregate together. Each humped, craggy, and gleaming individual is unique. Heavy waves can break them off the rocks and wash them to shore.

Oysters congregate and permanently cement themselves to rocks, and their beds can be almost as large as mussel beds. However, oysters are generally less conspicuous than mussels because of their gray color and more rounded shape. Like other bivalves, oysters clean the water they live in by eating tiny particles. An adult oyster can filter up to 50 gallons of water a day. They are essential to a healthy coastline.

If a shell is flat, thin, and strange looking, it is probably a Pacific Oyster (*Crassostrea gigas*). A Pacific Oyster's shell is shaped something like a shoehorn, but it can come in a wide range of shapes and may have fluted or ruffled outer layers. Generally it is rectangular and about 6 inches long, but it can grow up to 1 foot in length. Pacific Oyster shells are usually gray but can range from white to black, and pink or yellow shells are not uncommon. In terms of shape, size, and color, this species is one of the most variable in Southern California. It is actually a western Pacific bivalve that was introduced from Japan about eighty years ago, and now it is raised commercially along the Southern California coast.

American Oysters (*Crassostrea virginica*) and California Oysters (*Ostrea lurida*) have thicker shells, but they are also irregularly shaped. The California Oyster is small, about 3 inches in diameter, rounded, and has a glossy greenish interior. The American Oyster can be 6 to 8 inches long. It has a white interior with a purple spot near the center of the shell. Each of these oysters has a large, deep shell that it cements to a rock. This shell contains most of the oyster's body, while the smaller flat shell sits on top and serves almost as a trapdoor, slamming shut when the creature needs to protect its fleshy body parts.

One of the fascinating things about oysters is their ability to change gender. An oyster may start life as a male, and then change to a female. Spawning can cause an oyster to change gender several times in its life.

Agate Jewel Box
(Chama arcana)

Pacific Oyster
(Crassostrea
gigas)

Left: *American
Oyster* (Crassostrea
virginica) Right:
California Oyster
(Ostrea lurida)

Boring Mya (*Platyodon cancellatus*)
Flat-Tipped Piddock (*Penitella penita*)
Rough Piddock (*Zirfaea pilsbryi*)

As you walk along the shore, you may see rocks that look as holey as Swiss cheese. Many people think erosion causes these holes, but they are actually burrows made by rock-boring bivalves. Some rock borers slowly twist and grind their shells into shale in a circular motion, while others rock their shells back and forth. Either way, their rough shells slowly drill a hole in the rock, which becomes their permanent home. As a borer grows, it enlarges its burrow by rocking and rolling its shell against the walls.

The 3-inch-long shell of the Boring Mya (*Platyodon cancellatus*) does not completely enclose the creature's siphon. Instead, the shell merely curves around the siphon like a small hamburger bun around an oversized hot dog. Like other rock borers, its valves do not have to close tightly because the rock home provides permanent protection.

The shell of the 3-inch-long Flat-Tipped Piddock (*Penitella penita*) looks as if it folds back on itself, creating triangular plates at one end of the piddock's shell. These extra layers of shell have rough surfaces, and the piddock uses them to grind away rock. The Flat-Tipped Piddock also has a paper-thin "sleeve" created by the mantle, which extends outside the shell to protect its siphon. You may find shells with this sleeve still attached, though when it dries it becomes very fragile and crumbles easily.

The Rough Piddock (*Zirfaea pilsbryi*) is larger and heavier than the other rock borers. It grows up to 6 inches long and burrows into clay and soft rock with its rough, pointed shell. The white shell has a sharp, filelike exterior that is indented in the middle and flares to a point on either end. Both ends gape open to accommodate the large body and siphon of this creature.

From the safety of its rock-walled home, a rock borer extends its siphon into the water to feed. When a rock-borer dies, its shell crumbles, and eventually the hole it lived in becomes a shelter for other creatures, such as anemones, small gastropods, fish, or crabs. You may find fragments or single valves of rock borers while beachcombing, but a whole shell is rare since it usually remains trapped or encased in the hole the rock borer made.

Boring Mya
(Platyodon
cancellatus)

Inset: *shale with
rock borer homes*

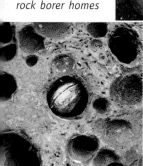

*Flat-Tipped
Piddock*
(Penitella
penita)

Rough Piddock
(Zirfaea pilsbryi)

POLYPLACOPHORA (CHITONS)

Mossy Chiton (*Mopalia muscosa*)

Polyplacophora is a class of mollusks that differs from all other mollusks. Chitons aren't considered univalves or bivalves because their shells are actually composed of separate segments or overlapping plates—*poly* means "many," *plac* means "plate," and *phora* means "bearer." The Pacific coast hosts almost a hundred different chiton species, but they are frequently overlooked because they blend well with rocks in the intertidal zone. A chiton looks like a rock, is segmented like a pill bug, and clings to rocks with its foot. Their shells can have beautiful natural patterns and colors, but the chitons that live in the intertidal zone are often eroded and dull, which makes identifying particular species very difficult. In some cases experts must rely on dissection to correctly identify a species. The Mossy Chiton (*Mopalia muscosa*) is easier to recognize because this 3-inch-long creature frequently has algae growing on its shell.

To find a chiton amid the rocks, look for a 1- to 3-inch long, oval shell composed of eight chevrons. If a predator pries a chiton from its rock, these chevron-shaped plates enable the chiton to curl up into a ball to protect its soft, meaty underside. When a chiton dies, its body decays and these plates drop off and may be mistaken for fragments of a mussel or other bivalve; however, each plate is shaped like a roof and has rounded edges.

Some chitons rasp a rock with iron-filled teeth, creating a $\frac{1}{16}$- to $\frac{1}{4}$-inch-deep home scar depression; these teeth occur on the underside of its body. This depression is a safe haven during low tides and during the day. At night chitons venture forth to scrape and eat algae, bacteria, and bryozoans surrounding them on their rocks, returning to their home scars as morning dawns.

The chitons are the oval-shaped rows of chevrons in this tidepool.

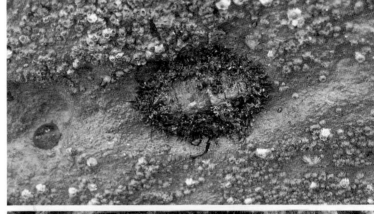

Live Mossy Chiton (Mopalia muscosa)

Fragments of Mopalia *species* showing chevrons

FLAT-SHELLED GASTROPODS (SNAILS)

By and large, rocky shores are dominated by gastropods. Many snails scrape algae off rock with a tonguelike conveyer belt of teeth called a *radula*. A gastropod has a head with eyes and antennae, and it is more mobile than bivalves. It can creep along on its "stomach-foot" (*gastro* is Greek for "stomach," and *poda* is Greek for "foot"). Most gastropods can be categorized into one of two informal groups: flat shelled and spiral shelled. The shell of a flat-shelled gastropod has subtle spirals, or they are absent altogether, and these animals look something like bivalves that are missing one shell. They use rock as their second valve, clamping to it for safety and to keep from drying out during low tides.

Pink Abalone (*Haliotis corrugata*)
Red Abalone (*Haliotis rufescens*)

The abalone is distinctively flat, oval, and ear shaped, and has small holes under the rim of its shell, which it uses to expel wastes, water, sperm, or eggs. Looking something like an upside-down pincushion, soft tentacles surround its body, and an adult has a very agile foot that it uses to grab drifting algae. Like most gastropods, the abalone's only defense is to clamp its shell to a rock.

There are several abalone species in Southern California, but only the Pink Abalone (*Haliotis corrugata*) and Red Abalone (*Haliotis rufescens*) are moderately common. The Pink Abalone grows about 8 inches long, the edge of its flat shell is scalloped, and there are corrugated bumps or ripples across its exterior. The Red Abalone can grow up to 1 foot long. Its reddish shell is lumpy but smoother than the Pink Abalone's. Often these species are coated with algae or other marine organisms, which grow on their shells, so it can be difficult to make out their color.

Wild abalones are no longer common, but they have a long history in California. Coastal Indians, such as the Chumash and Tongva tribes, used abalone shell for ornaments, fishhooks, and other tools, and harvested its meat for food. In the last fifty years pollution, overharvesting, and disease have taken a huge toll on these animals, particularly in Southern California, where their numbers have fallen alarmingly low. California has a small but thriving commercial abalone farm industry. Professional farms in the far-western Pacific now supply most of the abalone for restaurants and shells for manufacturing. Tourist shops sell the shells, and some shells are lacquered and used as small trays, or they are broken up and the fragments are used as mosaic pieces for tile and jewelry.

Red Abalone (Haliotis rufescens)

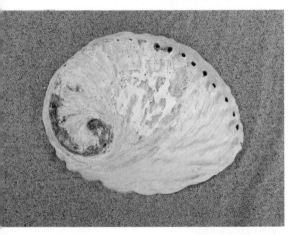

Exterior of Pink Abalone
(Haliotis corrugata)

Interior of Pink Abalone

Wild abalone is now protected, and collecting for any purpose is prohibited south of San Francisco. To get a good view of this beautiful creature, visit a coastal aquarium; some keep live abalones in touch tanks.

Rough Keyhole Limpet (*Diadora aspera*)
Volcano Limpet (*Fissurella volcano*)
Giant Keyhole Limpet (*Megathura crenulata*)

Limpets cling to every rock and line tidepools along the Pacific coast. These snails are divided into two main types: true limpets, which do not have a hole in their shells, and the keyhole species, which do. Although the presence of the hole appears to be the only difference between these two main types, they do differ internally. Both keyhole limpets and true limpets have a foot, a head with a radula for scraping algae, and gills. A keyhole limpet, however, expels waste, water, and spawn out the hole in the apex of its shell, like an abalone, which uses its side hole; a true limpet expels body fluids from under the mantle at the rim of its shell.

Most limpets live in the mid- to high intertidal zone, which means they are frequently exposed to sun and heat that dry and bleach their shells. Because they are sedentary, limpets can be eroded by sand, rocks, and wave action or covered with mineral deposits, algae, and barnacles. In addition, limpets that live in areas with rough water tend to have flatter and smoother shells, while limpets that dwell in calmer waters have rays and humps that are more distinct. All these factors make limpets difficult to identify.

In general, you can distinguish a keyhole species by the shape and location of its hole. The Rough Keyhole Limpet (*Diadora aspera*) has an off-center, but almost perfectly round, keyhole, and a grayish, 2- to 3-inch-long shell. A Volcano Limpet (*Fissurella volcano*) has an elongated hole, somewhat rectangular in shape, nearly in the center of its 1-inch-long shell. It may also have pink, purple, or coral-colored rays that look like lava running down the sides of a volcano. The Giant Keyhole Limpet (*Megathura crenulata*) has an oval hole rimmed with white. This species has a large body, too, that extends up and over its shell. It is very slippery, and predators have a difficult time gripping this limpet. The body extends well beyond the edges of its 5-inch shell, so a full-grown, live Giant Keyhole Limpet can be up to 8 inches across, making it the largest common snail on Southern California's rocky shores.

Rough Keyhole Limpets (Diadora aspera)

Volcano Limpets (Fissurella volcano)

Giant Keyhole Limpets (Megathura crenulata)

Giant Owl Limpet (*Lottia gigantea*)

Looking like oval outcroppings on rock, limpets appear to be completely stationary. But as the tide covers a limpet, the limpet lifts its shell a fraction of an inch and creeps along the rock surface on its stomach to forage. All limpets are herbivores. Each one rasps algae off rocks with its radula. It also uses its radula to create a depression in a rock called a *home scar,* which perfectly fits its body, and it can enlarge the home scar as it grows. Limpets use home scars like a second shell, for protection from sun, heat, and predators.

The Giant Owl Limpet (*Lottia gigantea*) is the largest North American true limpet. Some people describe it as the bully of the limpet world, since it can shove smaller species off rocks and defend the territory around its home scar. Its size, up to 3 inches, also makes it a handy platform for other creatures—such as other limpets, baby mussels, and barnacles—to attach to. In fact, if you see an oval-shaped cluster of barnacles on a bare rock, they are most likely attached to a Giant Owl Limpet.

Collectors often seek out large shells, but studies indicate that over the past hundred years the collection of large marine species has led to a reduction in the size of some marine gastropods. This can be partially explained by genetics: if people collect the large ones, only the small animals are left to pass on their genes to the next generation. This is one of the reasons there are laws against collecting tidepool animals.

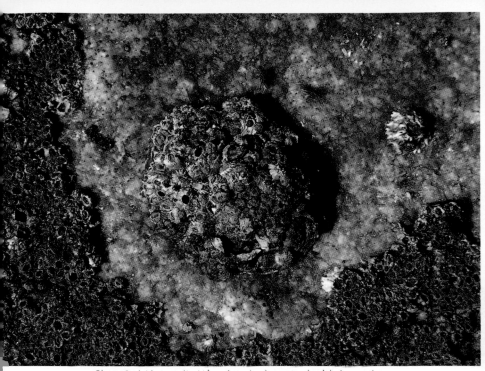

Giant Owl Limpet (Lottia gigantea) covered with barnacles

Giant Owl Limpet exterior (inset)
and interior (bottom)

Finger Limpet (*Lottia digitalis*)
Rough Limpet (*Lottia scabra*)
File Limpet (*Lottia limatula*)
White Cap Limpet (*Acmaea mitra*)

Most limpets are mottled gray and brown, but it is hard to say what their "normal" color is. Like the rocks they live on, limpets are subject to the deteriorating effects of erosion, wave action, and the sun, so they tend to take on the color of the rocks in their environment. The same salt deposits, algae, and microorganisms that cling to the rocks around them also cling to limpets. Because of this, it is easier to identify species based on shape rather than color.

Finger Limpets (*Lottia digitalis*) and Rough Limpets (*Lottia scabra*) are both egg shaped and about 1 inch long. A Rough Limpet has pronounced ridges from the apex of its shell to the rim, while a Finger Limpet is smoother with less-pronounced rays. The ½-inch-long File Limpet (*Lottia limatula*) is rounder, flatter, and smoother than the others in this book, and it has very faint rays.

In Southern California, File Limpets that lack normal pigmentation are fairly common. These albino File Limpets may be confused with the White Cap Limpet (*Acmaea mitra*), but albino File Limpets retain a tan spot or two, while White Cap Limpets are pure white inside and out. Moreover, White Cap Limpet shells (and the shell of their close relative the Kelp Limpet, *Discurria insessa*) are more peaked than the shells of *Lottia* species. Look for the White Cap Limpet in tidepools, grazing on Encrusting Coralline Algae (*Lithothamnion* species). This pretty pink alga grows in a stiff mat over rocks and sedentary creatures like the White Cap Limpet—a good way to escape being eaten!

Left: *Finger Limpet* (Lottia digitalis)
Right: *Rough Limpet* (Lottia scabra)

Albino File Limpet (Lottia limatula)

Inset: *normal File Limpet*

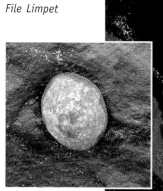

White Cap Limpets (Acmaea mitra)

Hooked Slippersnail (*Crepidula adunca*)
Onyx Slippersnail (*Crepidula onyx*)
Giant Slippersnail (*Crepidula grandis*)
Pacific Half-Slipper (*Crepipatella dorsata* or *C. lingulata*)

Although slippersnails look a bit like limpets, they are only distantly related. A slippersnail has two distinguishing features: a small hook at the apex of its shell, and a thin platform that fits across the underside of its shell. If you turn a slippersnail upside down, you will see why it received its common name. The platform's function is to protect the body of the snail, just as the inner spiral most gastropods have protects them.

Slippersnails ride piggyback on other shells and it is common to find small males piled on top of a much larger female. Some species live their entire lives like this. Since a slippersnail is mostly stationary, it captures food particles that pass by with its sticky mantle. Slippersnails begin life as males and gradually change into females as they grow larger, so the slippersnail at the bottom of a pile is likely a female—or soon will be! A female broods fertilized eggs for about a month before free-swimming young emerge from her shell and eventually settle into a sedentary life.

The Hooked Slippersnail (*Crepidula adunca*) is about ½ inch long, dark brownish blue, and has a distinct hook at its apex that flops over, making the shell look like the saggy hat of an elf. The Onyx Slippersnail (*Crepidula onyx*) has a sturdy 2-inch-long shell with a fairly strong, white platform. The shell is reddish brown on the inside and buff or tan on the outside. Some Onyx Slippersnails are flat and almost round, while others have raised oval shells. The 3-inch-long Giant Slippersnail (*Crepidula grandis*) has a mosslike periostracum coating its round shell. People refer to the shells of Pacific Half-Slippers (*Crepipatella dorsata* or *C. lingulata*) as *Cup-and-Saucer* shells for the small, round platform that only fully connects on one side of the shell. This species can be solid white or mottled tan on the outside, and it is glossy tan on the inside.

Hooked Slippersnail
(Crepidula adunca)

Giant Slippersnail (Crepidula grandis)

Onyx Slippersnail
(Crepidula onyx)

Pacific Half-Slipper
(Crepipatella
    dorsata *or*
    C. lingulata)

Chestnut Cowrie (*Cypraea spadicea*)

For thousands of years, people prized the spectacular cowries of the South Seas as money and jewelry, and even today many of these beautiful and rare species are expensive collector's items. The Chestnut Cowrie (*Cypraea spadicea*) is rather plain in comparison and is not nearly as interesting looking as its flashy relatives. Still, it is the only West Coast cowrie species in North America, and many beachcombers are delighted to find one.

The adult Chestnut Cowrie is unmistakable. Falling somewhere between flat shelled and spiral shelled, it has a smooth, reddish brown, hump-shaped shell, about 2 inches long, with "teeth" along its slit-like aperture, from which the snail's body emerges. The living animal has a large, spotted mantle that covers its shell, like eyelids, and when something startles the cowrie it quickly retracts the mantle, leaving the shell to "stare down" the predator. The mantle protects the Chestnut Cowrie from abrasion and helps rebuild the outer surface of the shell, keeping it coated with a gloss that remains for some time even after the cowrie has died.

Chestnut Cowries live all along the California coast, but they are most common south of Point Conception. They are scavengers and eat just about anything—anemones, carrion, sponges, and the eggs of marine snails. Since mussel beds trap oceanic debris, cowries like to graze in them, and you may find one cleaning up a tidepool near the subtidal zone. If you do not have any luck spotting this creature in the wild, there are marine aquariums all along the Southern California coast where you can see a Chestnut Cowrie up close.

Chestnut Cowrie (Cypraea spadicea)

SPIRAL-SHELLED GASTROPODS (SNAILS)

Spiral-shelled gastropods look more or less like garden snails, and they are fairly mobile. Some move freely along rocks eating algae, while others are predators that help control mollusk and other sea creature populations. Like all marine creatures, they are an important part of the food web. Some species broadcast eggs and sperm into the ocean where they become part of the oceanic plankton. Other snails mate and lay eggs in interesting designs—spirals, loops, blobs, or minute bulbs. Either way, the spawn of all snails is a vital food source for other creatures.

Eroded Periwinkle (*Littorina keenae*)
Checkered Periwinkle (*Littorina scutulata*)

Like sheep on a hillside, periwinkles graze over algae-covered rocks. These tiny marine snails, less than ½ inch long, are shaped like garden snails, but their shells are harder and can be checked, striped, or brightly colored green, brown, blue, and white. The two most common species in Southern California are virtually identical. However, Eroded Periwinkles (*Littorina keenae*) have duller colors, are rounder, and often have very worn shells. The Checkered Periwinkle (*Littorina scutulata*) has a slightly higher spire, and even when its shell is worn it retains some blue, green, or tan speckles.

Unlike some gastropods, periwinkles can tolerate very dry conditions and can survive for a couple of months stranded at the high tide line. This adaptation enables them to escape predatory sea stars and drill snails, which need a wetter environment. However, it leaves the periwinkle vulnerable to birds and crabs. To keep itself from drying out, a periwinkle—like most spiral-shelled gastropods—has a stiff disk called an *operculum* on the top of its foot. When it draws its foot into its shell, the disk plugs the aperture and protects the body of the snail, almost as the second valve of an oyster protects its soft body. Periwinkles also exude a sticky mucus, which glues them to rocks and helps seal their shells, enabling them to retain moisture for months until a tide covers them again. This ability to survive on dry land has led some researchers to believe that periwinkles are ancestors of land snails.

The periwinkle's habitat is cool and moist at low tide and protects the snail from the strongest waves. Rocks and tidepools in the high intertidal zone are ideal, and at low tide you usually can find a cluster of periwinkles hunched down in a shady crevice or a depression in a rock, waiting for the tide to come in. The incoming tide deposits a thin coating of microscopic algae, which the periwinkle scrapes with its radula as it slowly creeps over the rocks.

Periwinkles are tiny—less than ¹/₂ inch long. The shell in the center of all the periwinkles is an Eroded Periwinkle (Littorina keenae).

Checkered Periwinkles (Littorina scutulata) nestle in crevices during low tide.

Black Tegula (*Tegula funebralis*)
Brown Tegula (*Tegula brunnea*)
Banded Tegula (*Tegula eiseni*)

Tegulas have a couple of common names that are derived from their shape. Some people call them *top shells* because if you place a shell upside down on its spire, it looks like a toy top. They're also known as *turbans*. Tegulas resemble periwinkles but are considerably larger. They prefer wetter conditions than periwinkles, so you are more likely to find them in the mid- to low intertidal area, where they commonly graze on algae at the base of rocks. Tegulas broadcast eggs and sperm into the water without mating. The sex cells, fertilized eggs, and hatching larvae float in the water until the larvae develop enough to settle on the rocks.

Sand and sea often erode the layers of the Black Tegula's (*Tegula funebralis*) shell, exposing an orange tip and pearly layers along the shell's whorls. Shells that haven't been eroded fade to dull purple when dry. Except for color, the Brown Tegula (*Tegula brunnea*) is nearly identical to the Black Tegula, but it lives on floating kelp. Its shell may be eroded to pale yellow and white. The Banded Tegula (*Tegula eiseni*) has small bumps along its whorls, unlike Black or Brown Tegulas, which have smoother shells. All three species are about 1 inch in diameter.

It is difficult to identify tegula shells because they look very similar. The umbilicus of a gastropod can offer identification clues, though. The whorls of a snail spiral around a central axis that runs from the top spire to the base of the shell. The umbilicus is the opening of this axis; it's located next to the aperture. In some species the umbilicus is covered with a layer of shell, but the Banded Tegula has an umbilicus that looks like an "innie" belly button. Black and Brown Tegulas have a smooth umbilicus that looks like an "outie" belly button.

Keep in mind that sometimes seaweeds and some species of animals, such as hydroids and bryozoans, make their homes on tegula shells, and this, coupled with the effects of erosion, can make proper identification almost impossible. As frustrating as this can be, observing the behaviors of animals grazing and interacting in a tranquil tidepool can be just as satisfying as identifying and classifying every creature.

Black Tegula (Tegula funebralis)

Brown Tegula (Tegula brunnea)

Banded Tegula (Tegula eiseni)

A tegula covered with a bryozoan

Western Ribbed Top Shell (*Calliostoma ligatum*)
Wavy Turban (*Megastraea undosa*)

Blue Top Shell is another name for the Western Ribbed Top Shell (*Calliostoma ligatum*), but this name is a bit misleading. This snail's shell is actually brown with delicate, thin bands lining its whorls. However, hidden under its somewhat mundane exterior is a treasure of sparkling neon blue color, which is exposed where the outer shell has been eroded. The Western Ribbed Top Shell lives in deeper water than tegulas, but if you go exploring during a minus tide you may find them grazing along rocks or attached to kelp. Their shells are fairly common on rocky shores, and occasionally a hermit crab may be using one as a home.

Because of its large size and beauty, some people call the Wavy Turban (*Megastraea undosa*) *Queen Top Shell*. This spectacular-looking snail grows up to 5 inches across and 4 inches high. A wavy rope pattern parallels the bottom of each whorl like a ruffle on the bottom of a skirt. A rough translation of this creature's scientific name is "giant undulating star." The Wavy Turban's brownish top layer is often worn away, exposing a layer of iridescent pink and green mother-of-pearl. The shell may also be covered with Encrusting Coralline Algae (*Lithothamnion* species)—the pink alga that grows in tidepools and on the shells of slow-moving, rock-dwelling invertebrates. The Wavy Turban lives on rocks in the subtidal zone, but occasionally you might find it in tidepools at the very low intertidal zone, and in calm waters such as in the shallows under a dock. Many of the coastal aquariums or discovery centers have live specimens in their tanks, where visitors can get a close look at this strange and beautiful creature.

Western Ribbed Top Shell (Calliostoma ligatum)

Wavy Turban (Megastraea undosa)

Live Wavy Turban

California Frog Shell (*Bursa californica*)
Kellet's Whelk (*Kelletia kelleti*)

The California Frog Shell (*Bursa californica*) and Kellet's Whelk (*Kelletia kelleti*) are two large, spiral-shelled gastropods that live along rocky shores. They are unrelated but look similar. Since the beautiful yellow and tan California Frog Shell lives in the subtidal zone, it is unlikely that you will ever see this animal alive; however, its 2- to 3-inch-long shell or shell fragments commonly appear along rocky beaches, where they may be mistaken for Kellet's Whelk shells because they both have knobby whorls. You can identify the California Frog Shell by the pointed knobs on its whorls and the varix that forms a thick lip around the shell's aperture. Varices are areas where the shell is thicker; a gastropod creates them when it stops growing for a significant period of time. Varices transect the whorls like a rib, but they are much thicker and more irregular than ribs.

A gastropod grows from the peak of its shell, or *top spire,* down to its aperture. At one time its shell was as small as the tip of the top spire! You can trace the growth of a California Frog Shell by turning it in your hand. After the shell completes one full turn, or *whorl,* there is a varix, indicating a period of time when the snail stopped growing. When the snail resumed growing, it formed another whorl, which, in the case of the California Frog Shell, has pointed bumps. Every time a snail completes a whorl, it stops growing and forms another varix. This cycle of growth and nongrowth is repeated throughout the California Frog Shell's life, until it reaches its maximum length of about 4 inches.

A Kellet's Whelk grows nearly 7 inches long, though 4 to 5 inches is more common. It does not have varices, but it grows rounded knobs along its whorls. The aperture is elongated and has a graceful twist that is distinctive. The body of the creature is bright school bus yellow, and its shell is white or tan. However, pink and green algae, barnacles, and other marine organisms often live on its shell and make it difficult to discern its color. You can find Kellet's Whelks in tidepools and sometimes buried in wet sand at the base of a rock. This snail is a scavenger; it has an extremely long, retractable proboscis that looks like a flexible drinking straw. It probes the ocean floor and rocky crevices with this organ, which can extend over a foot in length, to get at food.

Although it is native to Southern California, the Kellet's Whelk has been migrating up the coast over the last twenty years and can be found as far north as Santa Cruz, where reportedly it has become part of the sea otter's diet.

California Frog Shell (Bursa californica)

Kellet's Whelk shell (Kelletia kelleti)

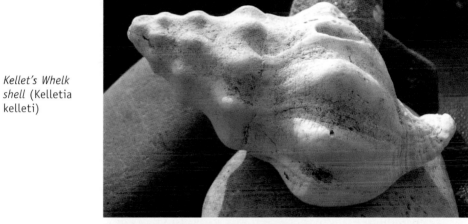

The foot of a Kellet's Whelk emerging with operculum visible

Unicorn Shell (*Acanthina* species)
Poulson's Dwarf Triton (*Roperia poulsoni*)
Atlantic Oyster Drill (*Urosalpinx cinerea*)

Tropical and deep-sea species of the murex family are large, showy, and very different from their humble-looking relatives—unicorn shells, Poulson's Dwarf Tritons, Festive Murex, and Dogwinkle—along Southern California shores. Members of this large and globally distributed family contain a purple dye that coastal peoples all over the world used to color cloth for royalty and the upper classes. If you find an empty murex shell, look for the trademark purple stain on its interior. All murex species are carnivores that eat a variety of creatures, including barnacles, snails, mussels, and other bivalves.

You may find hundreds of unicorn shells (*Acanthina* species) clustered under an overhanging rock in the intertidal zone, feeding on barnacles. Like all gastropods, they take on the coloration of rock as wind, waves, and sun age their shells, and small organisms, such as bryozoans, grow on them. This makes it difficult to identify unicorn shells beyond the genus classification. A unicorn shell has a tiny tooth or spine that sticks up on the lip of its aperture, which it uses to pry shells open. Some imaginative person decided it looked enough like a unicorn's horn to give this creature its common name. An older name for a unicorn shell is *thorn drupe*.

Poulson's Dwarf Triton (*Roperia poulsoni*) and the Atlantic Oyster Drill (*Urosalpinx cinerea*) have bad reputations as "oyster drills," and many people regard these ravenous little predators as pests. There are about six members of the murex family in Southern California that are commonly called dwarf tritons (*Ocenebra, Ocinebrina, Roperia,* and *Urosalpinx* species), though some of them are now known as *rocksnails.* Even though the largest species only grow to 1½ inches long, they can destroy commercial oyster beds—a single infestation of some species can cost an oyster grower her livelihood.

Each Atlantic Oyster Drill, like other marine snails, has a filelike radula, which it uses to drill into oysters. Other tritons and drill species are not so destructive, but all are carnivorous. The shell of a Poulson's Dwarf Triton has three whorls after the top spire, thin brown stripes that wind around the whorls, and five or six bumps, called *teeth,* on the lip of the oval aperture. The Atlantic Oyster Drill looks something like a Kellet's Whelk, though it only grows to ¾ inch long. Its shell is gray and tan with small knobs along its whorls and a flared lip at its opening that shows a purple interior. Look for tritons and drill snails along pilings as well as in tidepools.

Unicorn shells (Acanthina *species*)

Poulson's Dwarf Tritons (Roperia poulsoni) *surround an eroded Atlantic Oyster Drill* (Urosalpinx cinerea).

Festive Murex (*Pteropurpura festiva*)
Dogwinkle (*Nucella emarginata*)

The Festive Murex (*Pteropurpura festiva*) may be dark brown, yellow, or beige with brown stripes. Although the shells of the Festive Murex are frequently badly eroded, you should be able to see long, round ridges transecting the whorls from the top spire to the other end of the shell. The aperture is typical of species of the murex family: it does not extend to the tip of the shell, and it is surrounded by a thick lip that has small, rounded teeth.

The Dogwinkle (*Nucella emarginata*) lives on rocks near the high tide line. At first glance it may be mistaken for a tegula or large periwinkle, but it has thin grooves along its shell and a wider aperture. The Dogwinkle can be brown, black, yellow, or purplish. Its shape varies from round to more narrow and pointed, and the patterns on its shell may be striped, checked, or a solid color. Although its appearance varies widely, it is considered a single species.

Festive Murex (Pteropurpura festiva)

Dogwinkles (Nucella emarginata)

Purple Olive (*Olivella biplicata*)
California Cone (*Conus californicus*)

Although the Purple Olive and California Cone do not belong to the same scientific family, they look similar and share the same habitat, so people frequently confuse the two. However, a Purple Olive (*Olivella biplicata*) shell is shaped a bit like a football and has a narrow aperture. The California Cone (*Conus californicus*) is flared like an ice-cream cone, and it has a long, narrow aperture that nearly spans the length of its shell. Note the wide color variation (beige to purple) and size ($\frac{1}{2}$ to $1\frac{1}{2}$ inches long) of each species.

When people find a discarded olive snail (*Olivella* species) shell, there often is a perfectly shaped hole where its top spire was located. This means that the snail fell prey to a moonsnail, which drilled into the snail and ate it. California Cones also prey upon them, but they kill victims with a unique radula that is attached to a venom sac. This radula is shaped like a harpoon, and this snail injects poison into the body of its prey. These creatures are too small to hurt humans, but you should take care if you happen upon a live specimen. Larger gastropods, such as moonsnails, eat California Cones as well.

Both these snails remain buried in sand or among small rocks during the day and hunt at night. You are more likely to find the shells of these species along rocky shores, where hermit crabs use them as homes. Evidently, the crabs find these shells in the sand and carry them into the tidepool environment.

Purple Olive
(Olivella
biplicata)

*California
Cone* (Conus
californicus)

Purple Olive (left)
*and California
Cone* (right)

MOLLUSKS WITHOUT SHELLS (SEA SLUGS AND OCTOPUS)

California Brown Sea Hare (*Aplysia californica*)

Many unwary tidepoolers have accidentally touched a soft, slimy California Brown Sea Hare (*Aplysia californica*) and have been alarmed as the water turned royal purple, magenta, and hot pink. As startling as the color change might be, it's caused by completely harmless ink, which the sea hare releases to protect itself. The amount of fluid and the astonishing color seem out of proportion to such a nondescript creature, but it is an effective smoke screen that befuddles predators while the sea hare makes its getaway.

The California Brown Sea Hare belongs to an order of mollusks called *sea slugs* or *nudibranchs,* derived from the Latin *nudi,* meaning "naked," and *branchia,* meaning "gill." Many adult sea slugs don't have external shells, and they don't grow very large. The sea hare is different. It grows over a foot long, and it retains its small shell internally, growing a soft body around it as the sea hare matures. The sea hare has rounded hindquarters, something like a rabbit's, and it has long earlike antennae. People occasionally confuse it with the sea cucumber (*Parastichopus* species).

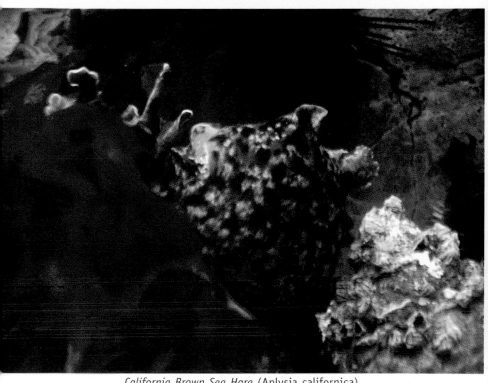

California Brown Sea Hare (Aplysia californica)

Black-Tipped Spiny Doris (*Acanthodoris rhodoceras*)
Sea-Clown Nudibranch (*Triopha catalinae*)
Spanish Shawl (*Flabellina iodinea*)
Horned or Opalescent Nudibranch (*Hermissenda crassicornis*)

Many sea slugs, or nudibranchs, are only 1 to 2 inches long. Their backs are covered with tiny, soft protrusions called *cerata* that can function as gills, aid the animal's circulatory system, serve as a defensive mechanism, and help camouflage the nudibranch. They can retract the cerata into their bodies. For example, the Black-Tipped Spiny Doris (*Acanthodoris rhodoceras*) rolls into a defensive ball when touched, and its cerata appear to be nothing more than black dots. Many nudibranchs are exquisitely colored, such as the orange and white Sea-Clown Nudibranch (*Triopha catalinae*). In addition to cerata, it has a rosette of orange-tipped gills on its hindquarters. The Spanish Shawl (*Flabellina iodinea*) is flamboyantly colored bright purple with an orange fringe, and the Horned or Opalescent Nudibranch (*Hermissenda crassicornis*) has a pale blue body with orange or brown cerata.

Diet varies with species, but nudibranchs feed on other soft-bodied creatures like sponges, hydroids, bryozoans, and anemones. After consuming a hydroid or anemone, a nudibranch can store the stinging cells of that creature in its cerata. This provides these soft-bodied animals some protection, because other creatures know that a nudibranch can be a nasty mouthful. Nudibranchs only live in tidepools—not on exposed rocks—in the low intertidal to subtidal zone, where they are less vulnerable to the sun during low tide. They reproduce by mating and lay eggs in beautiful patterns—spirals, chains, or loops.

Black-Tipped Spiny Doris (Acanthodoris rhodoceras) *rolled in a defensive posture*

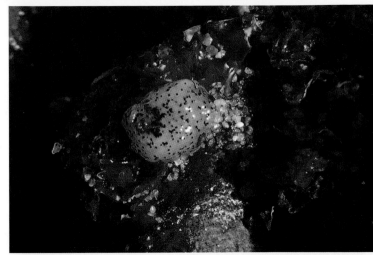

Left: *Sea-Clown Nudibranch* (Triopha catalinae)

Right: *Spanish Shawl* (Flabellina iodinea)

Horned or Opalescent Nudibranch (Hermissenda crassicornis)

Two-Spot Octopus (*Octopus bimaculoides*)

An octopus is more likely to see you than you are to see it. The Two-Spot Octopus (*Octopus bimaculoides*) is a shy, secretive, camouflage expert that seeks out cracks and crevices among rock piles to hide in. More adept than a chameleon, it can change color and alter the texture of its skin in order to blend with its surroundings; it can make itself bumpy to look like part of a rock formation, smooth to look like seaweed, or both to resemble a rock on sand. Although the deep-sea Giant Pacific Octopus (*Enteroctopus dofleini*) grows up to 30 feet long, the Two-Spot Octopus found along Southern California shores is much smaller—reaching only a foot or so in length. It is named for the two spots, which look like large blue eyes, on its hood near its tentacles. Don't be fooled, though, its real eyes are the two bumps on top of its head. Octopus eyes are so much like ours that medical students study them.

This amazing creature is related to the squid, cuttlefish, and nautilus, but according to researchers, octopuses are the most complex and intelligent of all mollusks. They figure out mazes and solve problems like how to get prey out of a closed jar. In addition, the octopus is an amazing escape artist that can squeeze through very small cracks and surround its prey with its delicate, searching tentacles before the prey realizes it. Female octopuses can go without food for months as they protect and care for their egg sacs. When the young finally hatch, the exhausted mother dies soon after. Octopuses are opportunistic feeders that will scavenge for prey as well as actively hunt fish, crabs, and snails. Its mouth has a small beak that bites through shells.

Many beachcombers naturally get very excited if they see an octopus, but they make the mistake of grabbing it and dumping it into a pail. This is stressful for the animal, and rough handling can rub off its slimy coating, which protects its skin from bacteria and disease. A better way to observe the octopus is to sit quietly near a low tidepool. Octopuses are intelligent and curious animals, and one may extend a tentacle to explore you if you are patient.

Two-Spot Octopus (Octopus bimaculoides) *photographed at Heal the Bay's Santa Monica Pier Aquarium*

Cnidarians

The cnidarian phylum includes radially symmetrical animals that don't have shells or skeletons. On rocky shores, the most obvious members of this phylum are anemones—cnidarians that stay in a plantlike polyp stage most or all of their lives (depending on the species). An anemone attaches its stalk end to a hard surface and extends its mouth end upward. Tentacles filled with stinging cells surround an anemone's mouth, and it is able to pull its tentacles closed around it. An anemone does this during low tide to retain moisture and protect the sensitive parts of its mouth.

ANEMONES

Aggregating Anemone (*Anthopleura elegantissima*)

Many marine species that occur along rocky shores don't look like what we think of as animals. For example, you may see a rock covered with broken bits of shell, sand grains, and small pebbles. Touch it gently and it may feel like the cold, jiggling surface of a bowl of Jell-O. If it does, Aggregating Anemones (*Anthopleura elegantissima*) are hiding under the debris. Their sticky skin collects shells and other small, hard fragments that keep their soft bodies from drying out. During low tide, the animals draw their brown and lavender tentacles into their stalks so that all that can be seen is the small debris. Each Aggregating Anemone can grow almost a foot in diameter, but 2 to 3 inches wide is far more common. Colonies made up of ½- to 1-inch-wide Aggregating Anemones can cover a boulder that is 10 to 12 feet across. These colonies are commonly called *anemone nurseries*.

If you gently stroke an anemone's tentacles, it will draw them in around its mouth—the hole in the center of its body. If the anemone does it quickly, it may surprise you with a small squirt of water that it shoots out of its mouth. Use the "one-finger rule" when touching anemones, and do not poke their mouths—this can injure them.

Anemones have stinging cells called *nematocysts* on their tentacles that help them capture prey. They are harmless to humans because the cells are not long enough or thin enough to penetrate our skin. Small animals and plankton, however, are not so lucky. The anemone traps them and draws them into its mouth. An Aggregating Anemone reproduces by fission, meaning its body divides, creating two identical anemones. Clusters of anemones are composed of genetically identical animals. According to researchers, spaces between anemones separate clonal groups with different genetics.

Aggregating Anemone (Anthopleura elegantissima) *colony covered with protective debris*

Aggregating Anemone clones

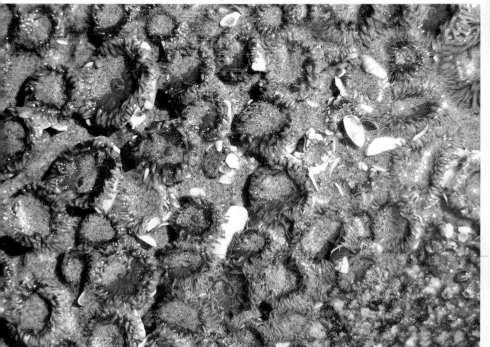

Sunburst Anemone (*Anthopleura sola*)

The Sunburst Anemone (*Anthopleura sola*) is a solitary creature that competes with other anemones that get too close; anemones will tangle tentacles and sting each other until one gives up and moves away. An anemone can move from place to place by releasing its grip on a rock and shifting its position by slow, infinitesimal degrees. They are able to move more rapidly by releasing from the rock and allowing the waves to carry them to better feeding grounds. On rare occasion you may see one tumbling in the surf on its way to a new home.

The beautiful Sunburst Anemone lives in and near the mid-intertidal zone, and if you look in an underwater cave or under a rock you may see one. It is named for the stripes that radiate from its centralized mouth. This species has interesting color variations and can range from nearly white to dark green. This color variation is caused by the amount of symbiotic algae in the anemone's tissue. During low tide, anemones completely contract their tentacles and look like nondescript blobs. This is a good time to admire an anemone's stalk, which is a freckled and mottled fleshy tube. When a wave washes over them, however, the anemones bloom, extending and waving their tentacles like children at a parade.

One of the creatures that preys upon anemones is the Wentletrap (*Opalia* species), a gastropod. Wentletrap is derived from the Dutch word for "staircase," and refers to the stair-stepped ribs that wind around this snail's spiral shell. If you examine an anemone closely, you may see a surprising number of these tiny creatures, less than $\frac{1}{2}$ inch long, burrowed near or under the anemone's stalk. Wentletraps spend their entire lives with anemones; they eat the stalks of anemones and can kill them. If you spot a Wentletrap away from an anemone, take a second look—it's probably just a shell being used by a small hermit crab.

A closed Sunburst Anemone (Anthopleura sola)

Sunburst Anemone color variation

Wentletrap (Opalia species)

Annelids

There are five phyla of worms and thousands of species in the marine environment. The annelid phylum is made up of segmented worms. Like earthworms, the bodies of marine annelids are made up of rings, or segments. Some marine annelids burrow in wet sand in the intertidal zone and are some of the creatures that sandpipers are hoping to catch as they probe the sand. The annelids that live on rocky shores, however, build tubes that encase and protect their bodies.

TUBE-BUILDING MARINE WORMS

Sandcastle Worm (*Phragmatopoma californica*)
Spiral-Tube Worm (*Spirorbis* species)
Calcareous Tube Worm (*Serpula columbiana*)

If you peek under the overhang of a submerged boulder, you may see hundreds of anemone-like plumes blossoming in the water. These are the tentacles of Sandcastle Worms (*Phragmatopoma californica*), a fascinating marine organism that lives in a tube of sand it makes. It grabs sand particles, covers them with mucus, then spits them out around its body. An individual tube is 3 to 5 inches long with a diameter of about ½ inch, but hundreds of these worms congregate and create "sand castles" several feet high and up to 6 feet wide. At low tide a castle looks like a giant honeycomb of sand. At high tide it blooms with lavender tentacles as the worms scoop food particles from the water.

There appears to be safety in numbers. Researchers believe that each additional tube strengthens the colony and helps support each worm's weight. Although a misplaced or careless step can easily destroy a colony, the design and placement of the castle is optimal for surviving the wash and pull of ocean waves. Look for Sandcastle Worms on rocky shores where both sand and rocks occur, or under breakwater rocks and along wharf pilings. They may even surround anemones and barnacles.

The spiral-tube worm (*Spirorbis* species) builds a hard mineral shell, like a snail's shell, and this worm may be mistaken for a young or minute Scaly Tube Snail (*Serpulorbis squamigerus*). These worms are so tiny that you may find more than a hundred of their white, coiled shells clinging to a 1-inch-long kelp float. They permanently attach their tubes to any handy surface, such as rocks, shells, or seaweed. An individual tube is about ¼ inch in diameter, and the worm inside each tube has tentacles that it uses to scoop microorganisms from the water.

The Calcareous Tube Worm (*Serpula columbiana*) builds a similar, shell-like tube, but its tube is larger, 2 to 3 inches long, and is not coiled. You can find the random squiggles of its tube attached to rocks and shells, like icing piped on a cake by a drunk baker.

Sandcastle Worms
(Phragmatopoma californica)

Spiral-tube worms (Spirorbis *species)*
on a kelp float

Calcareous Tube Worm
(Serpula columbiana) *tubes*

Sandcastle Worm
outside of its sand tube

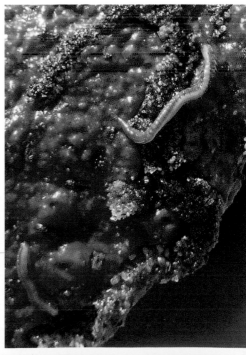

Arthropods

BARNACLES

Volcano Barnacle (*Tetraclita rubescens*)
Acorn Barnacle (*Balanus* species)
Buckshot Barnacle (*Chthamalus dalli*)

Almost every rock, piling, and tidepool along a shore has a barnacle on it. Though they look something like keyhole limpets, these abundant creatures aren't mollusks, they are crustaceans, which means they are related to crabs and lobsters. Within a barnacle's white, reddish, or gray shell is a little creature with jointed legs and an exoskeleton. Barnacles build their own shells, and they can't survive outside of them.

The shells of some barnacle species look like eroded volcanoes, such as the aptly named Volcano Barnacle (*Tetraclita rubescens*). Others, like acorn barnacles (*Balanus* species), have white or pink rays and grow up to 1 inch across; while still other species, such as the Buckshot Barnacle (*Chthamalus dalli*), are miniscule enough to be mistaken for lime or salt deposits. They are less than ⅛ inch high and ¼ inch in diameter. All of these shells are adaptations that help barnacles camouflage themselves; indeed, people easily overlook or mistake them for other species such as snails, gravel, or the ragged edges of rock. In fact, barnacles were classified as snails until the twentieth century, and people thought their legs were tentacles. Unlike keyhole limpets, barnacles often cluster together, like a carpet over a rock or wallpaper up a piling. And if you look closely at these surfaces, you will see the holes where the little creatures live. Barnacles can tolerate very dry conditions by remaining in their shells, so they can survive in the upper intertidal zone and nearly anywhere there is a solid substrate, including the shells of other animals, such as sand dollars, crabs, and limpets. Some species can even live on whales.

Barnacles stand on their heads and extend their legs into the water to feed. Their legs look like long false eyelashes, and the little brushes that line them capture microscopic food particles, which the barnacle pulls into its shell where its mouth is hidden.

Volcano Barnacle
(Tetraclita
rubescens)

Acorn barnacles
(Balanus *species*)

Inset: *red acorn
barnacles*

*Buckshot
Barnacles*
(Chthamalus
dalli) *on a limpet*

Pelagic Barnacle (*Lepas anatifera*)
Goose-Neck Barnacle (*Pollicipes polymerus*)

Pelagic Barnacles (*Lepas anatifera*) are a study in survival; you can find them attached to almost anything that floats, including kelp, molted feathers, and clumps of tar that bubble up out of the ocean floor and float on the surface of the Pacific, commonly drifting to shore. And unfortunately, you can also find them attached to foam cups, plastic, and other litter that floats in Southern California waters. Even though Pelagic Barnacles spend their lives drifting on oceanic currents, they frequently wash ashore, especially during spring and autumn when the seasonal currents change. They cannot survive for long stranded on a beach because they depend on drifting currents to bring them food.

Pelagic Barnacles have very flat, gray triangular shells that are about as thick as a fingernail. These shells perch atop slender, translucent stalks that enable them to bend and shift with the waves, which helps them feed. A full-grown Pelagic Barnacle can be 6 inches long, including its shell, but it is more common to find younger ones that are less than ½ inch long.

Both Pelagic Barnacles and Goose-Neck Barnacles (*Pollicipes polymerus*) are unusual in that they do not build hard, snail-like shells like other barnacles. Their shells are composed of plates that feel like fingernails. Sometimes people mistake Pelagic Barnacles for young Goose-Neck Barnacles, but the latter are coastal animals, and they are much larger. They grow flexible, fleshy stalks, 8 to 12 inches long, that end in rounded, pearly white "beaks." These beaks have bright red edges, and it looks as if the Goose-Neck Barnacle is wearing lipstick. Many people like the stalks, which taste like steamed clams, and they are standard fare in some seafood restaurants. Fishermen routinely use them for bait, so it is a good thing that this species reproduces prolifically. Goose-Neck Barnacles occur in mussel beds along the coast, where they form sizable rounded clumps composed of dozens and even hundreds of separate animals. When waves wash over them, their eyelashlike legs emerge to scoop food from the water.

Pelagic Barnacles (Lepas anatifera)

Goose-Neck Barnacles (Pollicipes polymerus)

ISOPODS

Western Sea Roach (*Ligia occidentalis*)
Scavenging Isopod (*Cirolana harfordi*)

In many ways the Western Sea Roach (*Ligia occidentalis*) resembles a cockroach—waving antennae, scurrying movements, scavenging habits—and so sometimes arouses the same repulsion people feel about its land relative. But this creepy 1-inch-long fellow is an essential scavenger of rocky habitats. The Western Sea Roach keeps harmful bacteria in check by eating decaying plant and animal debris that collects in the rocks and crevices along the shore, creating a healthier environment for all beachgoers. In addition, it is food for other creatures. Sea roaches are gray, but the shade darkens or lightens in response to light or heat.

The sea roach is well adapted to life on land, but it has gills that it must keep moist in order to breathe. It dips its gills in puddles and then, figuratively speaking, holds its breath as it goes about its business on land. Almost every protected rocky shore has these creatures, and sea roaches are active day and night. In a protected environment, such as Cabrillo Beach at San Pedro, you do not even need to turn over a rock to see a sea roach; they boldly sun and posture on top of them. Of course, if you try to get close they vanish in a flash, just like cockroaches.

The Scavenging Isopod (*Cirolana harfordi*) is less than 1 inch long and very secretive as it goes about its job efficiently cleaning up the tidepool habitat. In fact, Scavenging Isopods are so efficient at devouring every food scrap they find that sometimes scientists use them to clean the meat off bones that they are studying. A Scavenging Isopod is gray or brown and has a translucent tail that is rounded like a shrimp or lobster tail, rather than forked like a Western Sea Roach's tail. During low tide, you can find them swimming in tidepools or clinging to the underside of wet rocks.

Like other types of crustaceans, isopod exoskeletons are made up of hard, segmented plates. Some crustaceans have legs that are differentiated, meaning some of their legs collect food while other ones are used for walking. Isopod legs are undifferentiated; they use all seven pairs for walking, and they stick out from the sides of the Scavenging Isopod like skinny oars.

Western Sea Roach (Ligia occidentalis)

Scavenging Isopod (Cirolana harfordi)

HERMIT CRABS

Blueband Hermit Crab (*Pagurus samuelis*)
Hairy Hermit Crab (*Pagurus hirsutiusculus*)

Unlike most crabs, a hermit crab's body is soft rather than hard. To protect themselves, these crabs make their homes in leftover snail shells. A hermit crab clutches the inside whorls of a shell with the coiled end of its body. Hermit crabs have to find ever-bigger shells as they grow, and sometimes they duel for shells. A larger hermit crab may even bully a smaller crab out of its shell.

During summer you are apt to find dozens, even hundreds of hermit crabs scuttling around tidepools, looking like snails with legs. The larger Blueband Hermit Crab (*Pagurus samuelis*) favors rounded shells, like those of tegulas, while Hairy Hermit Crabs (*Pagurus hirsutiusculus*) prefer shells that are more pointed, like those of unicorn shells. Very young hermit crabs can even live in the minute shells of Wentletraps (*Opalia* species). Some hermit crabs try to fit their bodies into bits of garbage, a sad commentary on some beach environments.

All hermit crabs are fairly shy, and when disturbed they will retreat into their shells leaving only a claw peeping out. Hairy Hermit Crabs, however, are bolder than Blueband Hermit Crabs, and they will adjust much faster to a human picking them up. They are also more likely to nip your hand if they feel threatened. Bluebands are generally thinner and slightly more delicate looking than Hairy Hermit Crabs, though the two look very similar. Bluebands have tiny bright blue stripes on their legs. Hermit crabs have home territories, so if you pick one up it is important to place it back exactly where you found it.

Blueband Hermit Crab (Pagurus samuelis) *in tegula shell*

Hairy Hermit Crab (Pagurus hirsutiusculus) *in unicorn shell*

TRUE CRABS

Rock Crab (*Cancer* species)
Striped Shore Crab (*Pachygrapsus crassipes*)

Although crabs scuttle in and out of each tidepool and crevice along rocky shores, waving their claws at each other as they jostle for the best territory, they can be amazingly difficult to spot. They can squeeze into very small cracks in rocks, and you may not even be aware they are near. But if you crouch near a pile of rocks and listen, you may hear something that sounds like millions of microscopic bubbles popping. That faint popping or clicking is the sound crabs make as they feed, signal each other, and move along the rocks. If startled, a crab will retreat to the nearest crevice, face any would-be attacker with its claws out, and blow bubbles. Sometimes crabs create a net of bubbles that nearly conceals them. It's a strange and comedic defense mechanism, but as a communication tool and strategy for dealing with predators, it works well.

Crabs have gills and spend half their time in water and half on land. Like all crustaceans, the Rock Crab (*Cancer* species) and Striped Shore Crab (*Pachygrapsus crassipes*) are covered with a stiff shell called an *exoskeleton*. Eventually, a crab outgrows its shell and casts it off, revealing a soft, new one, which quickly hardens. The cast-off shells of *Cancer* crab species are common finds on the beach, especially the Rock Crab's reddish top shell, or *carapace*. The largest may be the size of a hand; the smallest may be smaller than the tip of a finger.

Striped Shore Crabs are very common in tidepools and along rocks. These beautiful creatures have bright green and black stripes, and adults have startling red claws. Unlike the similar Rock Crab, the Striped Shore Crab has wide-set eyes located on the front corners of its carapace. This crab's eyes roll constantly as it delicately picks at algae and conveys bits of it to its mouth with its claws. Eye rolling makes the crab appear comical, or as if it's bored with its dinner, but most likely the crab is watching for predators, waves, or competition.

Rock Crab
(Cancer *species*)
carapaces

Rock Crab

Striped
Shore Crab
(Pachygrapsus
crassipes)

Echinoderms

SEA STARS

Pacific or Ochre Sea Star (*Pisaster ochraceus*)
Bat Star (*Asterina miniata*)

At low tide you can find sea stars along the base of mussel beds, some-times half buried in wet sand as they wait for the tide to come in. Many people call these creatures "starfish," just as they call clams "shellfish," but *sea star* is more accurate for these star-shaped echinoderms. Many Pacific Sea Stars (*Pisaster ochraceus*) are orange and are called *Ochre Sea Stars;* however, this same species can also be purple or maroon. It's common to find sea stars of many shades in Southern California huddled together in large tidepools or clinging to the bases of rocks. They grow to over a foot in diameter.

Some sea stars eat plants, but the Pacific Sea Star is predatory, eating the mussels it lives among. It "stalks" its prey, walking on its hundreds of tube feet that resemble suckerlike disks. It clamps its prey with suckers and slowly pries the mussel's valves apart—just enough to ooze its stomach into the crack. The sea star's stomach juices soften and digest the mussel, and when the sea star retracts its stomach, the digested mussel goes with it.

A sea star clings tightly to a rock if a predator attacks it. In fact, a predator may pull off one of the sea star's arms (also called *rays*) before the sea star will loosen its grasp. A sea star can regenerate limbs, though, but it stresses the creature. If you run a finger along a sea star's back, you may be surprised at how dry it feels, even under water.

The Bat Star (*Asterina miniata*) is an omnivore; its habitat is algae and rocks covered with sea grass near the subtidal zone. It is about 5 to 7 inches in diameter when fully grown and occurs in a variety of colors, from orange to rosy red to bright purple. It is named for the webbing that connects its arms. Sea stars usually have five arms, but it's natural for them to have as few as four or as many as seven or eight.

Although sea stars don't have eyes, researchers have found that some species have light sensors on top of their rays that apparently help these creatures sense light and dark, and even the shadows of obstacles. Researchers are using this information to try to create artificial eyes for medicine and industry.

Pacific or Ochre Sea Stars (Pisaster ochraceus)

The mouth
and stomach
of a sea star.

Bat Star
(Asterina miniata)

SEA URCHINS

Purple Urchin (*Strongylocentrotus purpuratus*)
Red Urchin (*Strongylocentrotus franciscanus*)

The sea urchin, another echinoderm that lives in protected tidepools, is a hard, spiny ball that "walks" by rolling on the tips of its spines. This creature is more active than other echinoderms. It is more mobile than the sand dollar and faster than the sea star. I use "faster" loosely, as a sea urchin's top speed is only a few inches a minute. Like its relatives, sea urchins have tube feet—long, thin tentacle-like strands that stick out between their spines and help them maneuver.

Urchins are not related to anemones, though some people confuse them. Both are round and spiny, but the sea anemone has a soft body and is attached to a substrate, while the urchin is mobile and as hard and spiky as a fat, round sand dollar. Like the sand dollar, a sea urchin has a beaklike mouth and specialized jaw called *Aristotle's lantern* hidden among its spines. However, unlike the omnivorous sand dollar, most urchins stick to a diet of kelp and other algae. Underneath its spines a sea urchin has a pale, knobby shell called a *test*. The test is fragile, and it is uncommon to find a whole test, although you may find fragments along the shore. Look for thin green, white, or purple shells with a pattern of small studs and circles.

Purple Urchins (*Strongylocentrotus purpuratus*) have short purple spines, and are more common in tidepools than the Red Urchin (*Strongylocentrotus franciscanus*). Red Urchins live near and in the subtidal area, near kelp. They have longer spines and are commercially fished for the sushi market because their reproductive organs are considered a delicacy. In large numbers, urchins can destroy kelp beds with their voracious appetites, so some culling is probably beneficial to their habitat.

Purple Urchin (Strongylocentrotus purpuratus)

Red Urchin (Strongylocentrotus franciscanus). *The spines appear wavy because of ripples in the water.*

Sea urchin tests

SEA CUCUMBERS

California Sea Cucumber (*Parastichopus californicus*)
Warty Sea Cucumber (*Parastichopus parvimensis*)

The sea cucumber may be the strangest of all echinoderms. People often mistake this animal for a sea slug, but the sea cucumber is not related to mollusks in any way. Oddly enough, its closest relative is the sea urchin. The sea cucumber's skin feels leathery, because under its skin it has ossicles—microscopic particles that researchers believe are the remnants of a hard exoskeleton. The loss of all but the thinnest part of this rigid outer covering makes the sea cucumber the most flexible of all echinoderms. Like all echinoderms, sea cucumbers have tube feet, and they have spikes. Sand dollars and urchins have spines made of shell, but sea cucumbers have thorns, or spikes, made of thick skin. Both spines and spikes help deter predators.

The sea cucumber's body plan is very simple: a mouth surrounded by modified tube feet that act as tentacles, feeling for and grasping food; a long tubelike body; and a hind end that expels wastes. When it is frightened or in danger, the California Sea Cucumber (*Parastichopus californicus*) can also expel its intestines through this opening. Besides being alarming, the guts can confuse a predator—or become food for it—often allowing the sea cucumber to escape death. Within a month or two it can regrow its guts, but during this period of regrowth the animal is very stressed and more vulnerable to predation. The California Sea Cucumber has thorny spikes up and down its body and can grow up to 2 feet long.

The Warty Sea Cucumber (*Parastichopus parvimensis*) grows up to 1 foot long and is orangish brown with tiny black warts covering its surface. California and Warty Sea Cucumbers eat ocean-bottom debris and can be found in or near the subtidal zone, where both rocks and sand occur together.

California Sea Cucumber (Parastichopus californicus)

Warty Sea Cucumber (Parastichopus parvimensis)

Chordates

BONY FISH

Opal Eye (*Girella nigricans*)

If you sit motionlessly by a tidepool for a few minutes, tiny fish may grow accustomed to you and dart out and go about their business. Some species live in tidepools their entire lives, but tidepools are also nurseries for juvenile fish of larger species.

Juvenile Opal Eyes (*Girella nigricans*) are the most active, interesting, and complex creatures in Southern California tidepools. Behavior that seems like play to us can give you a glimpse of important survival strategies that they will carry into adult life. Young Opal Eyes hide under rocks and dart out when another fish swims by, then turn tail and dash off if the other gives chase. They often form little schools and may gang up on a crab, nosing and nibbling at the organisms that may be attached to its shell until the crab turns on them; then they all take off and hide under a rock. Sometimes these fish will slowly brush by each other, actually touching sides. It's fun to watch the antics of these young fish and try to figure out the reasons behind their behavior and how these behaviors might benefit them in the future.

When young, the Opal Eye is a common denizen of tidepools. You can easily identify it by its sleek, gray scales and a pearly white dot on its upper back. Almost 1 foot long when fully grown, the Opal Eye stays in a tidepool for a year or two, until it is large enough to migrate to its adult habitat, the kelp forest.

A baby Opal Eye (Girella nigricans)

Adult Opal Eyes —Phillip Colla/oceanlight.com

Tidepool Sculpin (*Oglicottus maculosus*)
Bay Pipefish (*Syngnathus leptorhynchus*)

The Tidepool Sculpin (*Oglicottus maculosus*) is another common resident of tidepools, but this fish is so well camouflaged that it is somewhat difficult to spot. Fully grown, it is only 3 to 4 inches long and has mottled brown, red, and beige spots. Its fins are flat with rays, and the Tidepool Sculpin holds them out from its body like a strange set of wings, making this a distinctive fish. The Tidepool Sculpin also has a triangular snout. Sculpins eat small crustaceans or scavenge the tidepool floor for ocean debris.

The long, skinny Bay Pipefish (*Syngnathus leptorhynchus*) rests and swims in an upright position. This straw-shaped fish sucks tiny organisms from the water while camouflaged among the bright green strands of eelgrass growing in the sand of some tidepools. The pipefish is a close relative of the seahorse, and the male has a pouch made of modified scales in which it broods its young, just like seahorses. One female—sometimes several females—will deposit her eggs in a male's pouch, and over the course of two to three weeks the male looks increasingly "pregnant" as the fertilized eggs develop and hatch into larvae. Juveniles emerge from the pouch looking like tiny threads, and they settle into the eelgrass to continue this creature's fascinating life cycle.

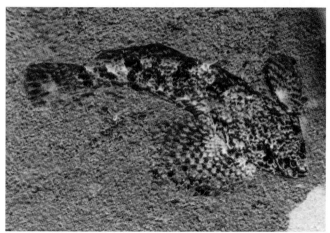

Tidepool Sculpin (Oglicottus maculosus)

Bay Pipefish (Syngnathus leptorhynchus) *in eelgrass*

Nearshore Waters

Besides offering an exciting place to swim and surf, Southern California's nearshore waters contain an amazing assortment of creatures, some of which are among the most unusual in the world. The nearshore waters are the threshold of the vast Pacific Ocean; and since there are enough marine species in this ocean to fill many volumes, I am only able to include a small sample of the creatures that I think are especially common or colorful, or have a unique life cycle.

Exploring the nearshore region can be as fun as going on a grunion run or taking a harbor cruise to get a closer look at marine mammals. Besides chance encounters while wading or swimming, snorkeling and scuba diving are options in some areas. And a fishing trip or discussion with the anglers that line the piers can provide you with interesting information about marine wildlife. Best of all, there are local marine centers along the coast in every county, where you can learn more about coastal wildlife and see underwater species up close. The options are broad and the rewards many, and once you know what to look for, you will be surprised at how often you find evidence of even the most elusive creatures—and sometimes the creature itself.

When entering the water, every swimmer and wader should do the "stingray shuffle." Instead of lifting your feet, shuffle or drag them along the ocean floor. This stirs up sand so that flat fish, rays, and other creatures can get out of your way without feeling threatened. Some rays have stingers or thorns that you will want to avoid.

Also, keep in mind that the Marine Mammal Protection Act prohibits any action that could even potentially disrupt a marine mammal's behavior patterns. Stay at least 50 feet from seals and sea lions. If you happen across a stranded marine mammal, contact a lifeguard for advice.

People recreating in the nearshore waters at Venice Beach

Surfing at Venice Beach

Plankton

Plankton is the umbrella term for the trillions of plants and animals that float in the sea. Plankton is a particularly appropriate name since it is Greek for "wanderer," and these organisms are unable to do more than float or swim feebly. *Phytoplankton* is the term for plant and algae cells that are part of the ocean's plankton; planktonic animals are called *zooplankton*. Single-celled animals; minute spawn and larvae; gelatinous sea creatures, like salp; and small crustaceans, such as krill (*Euphausia superba*), are all part of the ocean's zooplankton. Krill eat phytoplankton, and because they graze directly on primary producers, they are an efficient source of energy for larger animals, including whales.

PHYTOPLANKTON

Phytoplankton is composed of algal cells. Scientists refer to these cells as *primary producers* because they access sunlight energy for photosynthesis. In this process, phytoplankton uses the sun's energy to recombine molecules of carbon dioxide and water into food while expelling oxygen. In fact, phytoplankton produces dissolved oxygen, which is essential for the health of oceanic organisms, and the majority of the earth's breathable oxygen. Diatoms and dinoflagellates are some of the most prolific phytoplanktonic organisms. Although they cannot be seen without a microscope, diatoms are in every drop of ocean water and on every damp surface of the shore.

Diatoms and dinoflagellates are among the most beautiful single-celled entities on earth. Each one is surrounded by a sheer glass box, or "shell," made of silica. These shells have stunning, kaleidoscopic designs. Diatoms merely drift with the currents, but dinoflagellates seem to have a foot in both the plant and animal kingdoms since they can swim weakly with two taillike whips that set them spinning. Imagine if flowers could take wing to follow the sun!

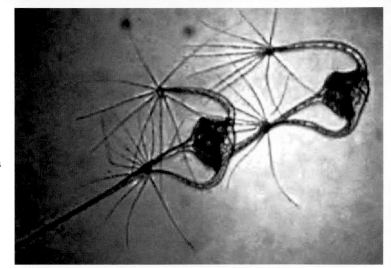

*Microscopic
dinoflagellates*
—Photo courtesy of
Gulf of the Farallones
National Marine
Sanctuary Photo
Library

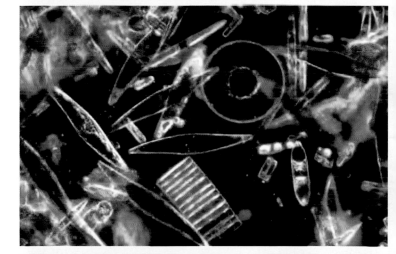

*Diatoms under
the microscope*
—Dr. Neil Sullivan
photo, courtesy of
NOAA

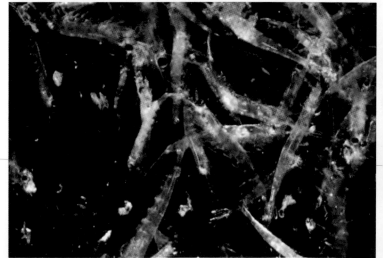

*Three- to five-
inch-long krill*
(Euphausia
superba) —Jamie
Hall photo, courtesy
of NOAA

RED TIDES

During spring and early autumn, there is a population explosion of phytoplankton, called an *algal bloom*. Also known as *red tides,* these events can turn ocean water brown and leave thick, soapy foam on the beach. Although not aesthetically pleasing during the day, at night phosphorescent species of phytoplankton glow along the waves and twinkle in the wake of every fish.

Zooplankton come to feed on the blooming algae; larger animals, such as fish, eat the zooplankton; and still larger creatures, such as sharks and marine mammals, feed on the fish. This oceanic orgy lasts for a few weeks. Then as the phytoplankton dies off, the bacteria that feeds on its dying cells uses up the oxygen in the water and the cycle ends. Sometimes the dissolved oxygen in the water is depleted so fast that fish suffocate in a massive die-off known as a *fish kill.*

At times species of diatoms that create domoic acid or dinoflagellates that create neurotoxins will bloom, and these toxins can build up in the creatures that eat them. Animals can carry these toxins all the way through the food web, poisoning marine mammals and humans. Neurotoxins tend to collect in the muscles of mollusks and cannot be cleaned out of the animal. Eating an affected mollusk can cause paralytic shellfish poisoning in humans. This is one of the reasons why there are seasonal restrictions on eating local shellfish in Southern California.

Algal blooms are a normal part of the ocean's cycle of life; however, in recent years the size and duration of them have increased, leading some scientists to believe that other factors, such as pollution and global warming, might be affecting the cycle of algal blooms in Southern California. This is of great concern because our health, in the context of available oxygen and the food we eat, depends on small planktonic organisms, which in turn are kept in balance by a healthy environment.

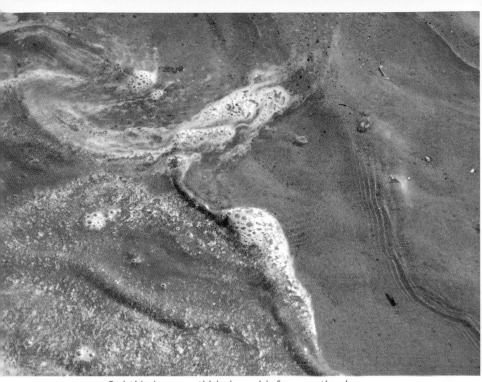

Red tide leaves a thick, brownish foam on the shore.

The brown water is the result of a red tide.

TUNICATES

Salp (*Salpa* species)

Transparency is the camouflage of the sea. It's as effective as a polar bear's white fur, enabling sea creatures to blend with their environments. All sorts of marine animals are clear, or nearly so, from krill, jellies, and the larval stages of fish, to mollusks and echinoderms. When sea creatures are young, soft gelatinous masses, transparency is even more vital to their survival. The salp (*Salpa* species), a clear, tube-shaped oddity, is one such creature.

Salps are tunicates, a subphylum of the chordate phylum, and like all tunicates each salp has a sleeve, or *tunic,* that covers and supports its body. At some stage in its development, a tunicate has a simplified spinal cord, and some species even look a bit like tadpoles. This means that of all the marine invertebrates out there, salps have more in common with vertebrates like us than all the others.

A lifelong denizen of the planktonic environment, the salp ripples the muscles that surround its body to swim weakly. It feeds continuously as it moves. Like a living piece of intestine, food goes in one end, travels through the body, and exits the other end. Salp sizes vary greatly—some species grow to 2 to 3 feet long, others are the size of footballs, and some species grow less than 1 inch long. In the ocean, some salp species fuse their tunics to each other to form spectacular glowing chains up to 100 feet long.

It is impossible to keep salps alive in even large aquariums, which makes them difficult to study. Unless you are a diver, the only place you are likely to see one is on the beach. Salps are driven ashore when currents change. Once stranded, they cannot survive because they need to be constantly moving in water. You may mistake a dead salp for the intestine of some animal or a piece of a jelly, but these simple creatures do not have tentacles and are completely harmless. If there is any question about what you have found on the beach, then do not touch it.

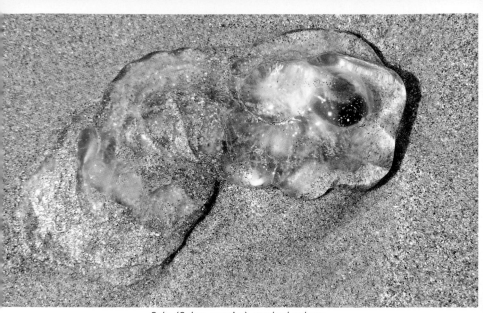

Salp (Salpa *species*) *washed ashore*

A pelagic salp chain
—Phillip Colla/oceanlight.com

Cnidarians

JELLIES

By-the-Wind Sailor (*Velella velella*)

Drifting with the currents and tacking with the wind, By-the-Wind Sailor (*Velella velella*) is one of the loveliest members of the amazing Cnidaria phylum. A couple of times a year you may see thousands of them stranded on beaches, but these small planktonic creatures, 3 to 4 inches across, spend their lives floating on the surface of the ocean. A By-the-Wind Sailor looks like a one-sail boat with a clear fin (the sail) rising from a disk-shaped body (the raft). Vivid bluish purple tentacles dangle from the rim of the disk.

By-the-Wind Sailor looks like a jelly or an upside-down anemone, but researchers believe that it is more closely related to hydroids because it has polyps, like a clam hydroid. If you can imagine the blooms of a rosebush as animate and actively performing different functions that benefit the rosebush as a whole, you can get an idea of how By-the-Wind Sailors work. The sail and raft of this creature make up its stalk, but the dangling "tentacles" are actually numerous polyps that have budded from the stalk. Different polyps have different jobs. Some are for reproduction, some harpoon prey with tiny stinging cells, and others digest food and spread the nutrients throughout the rest of the colony. By-the-Wind Sailor's stinging cells are too small to harm human hands; however, keep this creature away from your mouth, since your skin is more sensitive there.

These mysterious creatures are driven ashore by winds and currents; however, global weather and oceanic conditions are not the same from year to year. That's why some years there aren't any By-the-Wind Sailors, and other years there are large-scale stranding events. People easily overlook them on the beach because the sail and raft portions dry up and look like bits of cellophane or transparent autumn leaves. Once stranded, some of the fleshy purple polyps let go of the stalk as they are buffeted by the waves, birds on the shore eat others, and the rest vanish rapidly, melting away into the sand.

By-the-Wind Sailor (Velella velella)

Moon Jelly (*Aurelia labiata*)
Purple-Striped Jelly (*Chrysaora colorata*)
Sea Nettle (*Chrysaora fuscescens*)

Jellies are strange and beautiful bell-shaped cnidarians that drift or swim in nearshore waters. Many people call these animals "jellyfish," but they are not related to fish, so the more accurate term is simply *jelly*. Like anemones, jellies have a central mouth surrounded by tentacles that are armed with *nematocysts:* stinging cells that help capture and kill their prey. Contact with any object will trigger these tiny harpoonlike cells.

Small species, like the luminous Moon Jelly (*Aurelia labiata*), congregate in marinas and other quiet waters. A fringe of small tentacles hangs from the rim of its translucent dome, which looks like a shallow, inverted bowl. Moon Jellies with 4- to 6-inch diameters are quite common, but they can grow as large as 1 foot across.

You might encounter large, very toxic species such as the Purple-Striped Jelly (*Chrysaora colorata;* previously *Pelagia colorata*) and the Sea Nettle (*Chrysaora fuscescens*) in the surf, or they wash up on the beach where they look like plastic blobs on the sand. The Purple-Striped Jelly is huge—up to 2½ feet in diameter, though 1½ feet is more common—and has bright purple stripes across its dome. Instead of a fringe of tentacles hanging from its rim, the Purple-Striped Jelly has 6- to 10-foot-long tentacles that dangle from under the center of its dome. The dome of the Sea Nettle has a sparse fringe of tentacles; long tentacles also dangle beneath it and trail several feet behind this jelly as it drifts in the water. This species is yellow and orange and 8 to 12 inches in diameter.

Since a jelly cannot truly swim, it changes direction by flexing and contracting its dome, moving vertically up and down the water column. By moving up and down, it can find different currents, which can take it to a food source. Although jellies do not have eyes, they are light sensitive, and many spend the day deeper in the water and night at the surface. Jellies have amazing life cycles. When a fertilized egg hatches, the tiny larva attaches to a hard surface and resembles a plant with a stalk and a bulblike polyp. During the polyp stage, the larva is shaped something like an anemone. It grows and matures until it buds into many tiny jellies; this is called the *medusa stage*. The jellies break loose and float away to begin the life cycle anew.

You must take care to avoid jellies. Whether in water or washed ashore, the sting of even a dead jelly can be as painful as tangling with a nest of bees. If stung, use a towel or cloth to remove any tissue that

Moon Jelly
(Aurelia labiata)

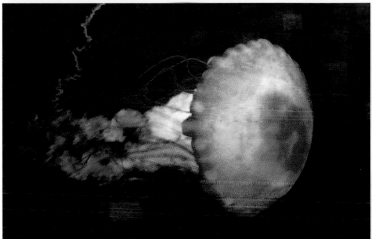

Sea Nettle
(Chrysaora
fuscescens)

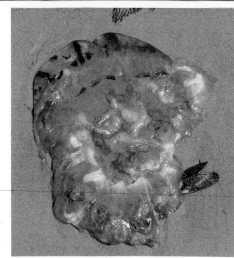

is stuck to your skin. Like bee stings, jelly stings are painful, but they are usually not life threatening, though some people may suffer a severe allergic reaction and should seek medical attention. If you find a stranded jelly, carefully bury it in the sand to prevent injuries to other beachgoers.

Purple-Striped Jelly on beach
(Chrysaora colorata)

Arthropods

LOBSTERS AND CRABS

California Spiny Lobster (*Panuliris interruptus*)
Sheep Crab (*Loxorhynchus grandis*)

Like a Don Quixote of the ocean floor, the heavily armored, 1-foot-long California Spiny Lobster (*Panuliris interruptus*) looks like it's waving two lances above its head as it walks along the ocean floor. Don't let this crustacean fool you—its lances are actually sensitive feelers, and if threatened, the lobster can jet backward to the safety of a crevice. It draws its tail to its underside, and the resulting jet of water propels it backward. The California Spiny Lobster only comes out to scavenge for food. And no wonder! Although it lacks the huge claws of its Atlantic Ocean cousin, it is still favored prey of fishermen, octopuses, sharks, sea lions, and seals. Lobster pots dotting the nearshore waters attest to this creature's popularity. Fishermen lower baited containers to the seafloor, and the lobsters, always looking for new territory and food, climb into them and are trapped.

The crusty-shelled Sheep Crab (*Loxorhynchus grandis*) is another armored denizen of rocks and crevices on the ocean floor. It is a member of the spider crab family; members of this family have round bodies perched atop long legs, making them look like oceanic spiders. The Sheep Crab has a thick, light-colored shell and two horns over its eyes. Although it looks fierce, it daintily tiptoes along the ocean bottom, plucking algae from rocks or scavenging the debris left by other predators. The Sheep Crab's bumpy shell looks a bit woolly under water—enough to give it its common name. Its shell can be 8 to 10 inches wide, and with its long legs stretched out to its sides, the Sheep Crab may measure almost 2 feet across.

Like all crustaceans, the California Spiny Lobster and the Sheep Crab periodically molt their exoskeletons. As a crustacean grows, its exoskeleton gets too small, so a crab or lobster wriggles free and crawls out of it, like a snake shedding its skin. It takes a few hours for the new exoskeleton to harden, and during this time the crustacean is very vulnerable. You often find discarded exoskeletons on the beach; sometimes the lobster's long, spiky feelers will still be attached. Both of these species live in the subtidal zone, near the shore, but on a rare occasion you may find one in a tidepool.

California Spiny Lobster (Panuliris interruptus)

California Spiny Lobster carapace

Sheep Crab (Loxorhynchus grandis) *picked over by gulls*

Chordates

BONY FISH

Grunion (*Leuresthes tenuis*)

It's midnight and suddenly the surf is alive with slivers of moonlight as hundreds of silvery fish leap and slither up the shore with each incoming wave. The Grunion are running! In a behavior unique among fish, the female Grunion rides a wave onto the wet shore, drills into the sand, and lays thousands of eggs, which are fertilized by males that follow them.

Every two weeks during spring and summer, grunions gather at night in the surf along sandy beaches, waiting for the tide to turn so they can spawn. Grunion spawn times are tied to the tides, which are tied to the moon cycle. Tides are highest during the new moon and the full moon, and lowest during the quarter moons. By spawning shortly after full and new moons, grunion eggs can remain undisturbed by waves for a couple of weeks—the amount of time the young need in which to develop and hatch.

In an exciting midnight tradition, thousands of Southern Californians chase and capture the spawning fish. The "grunion run" is such a popular event that the state requires participants to purchase a fishing license, prohibits collecting in certain months to protect the species, and won't allow people to use equipment to catch Grunions—bare-handed catches only! The grunion run, however, is taking on a new dimension, thanks to programs held by local aquariums and conservation organizations. Researchers and educators teach people about the uniqueness of this fish and the fragility of its habitat. The result is that many people now collect Grunions, which may be exhausted and stranded by the spawning process, and return them to the sea. It's heartwarming to see people grapple with the slippery little fish in the dark and release them into the waves.

Grunion (Leuresthes tenuis) swimming up to the beach

The grunion run

Grunion

Salema (*Xenistius californiensis*)
Pacific Jack Mackerel (*Trachurus symmetricus*)
Barred Surfperch (*Amphistichus argenteus*)

Nearshore waters in Southern California glitter with schools of small silver fish species, such as the beautiful Salema (*Xenistius californiensis*) and the Pacific Jack Mackerel (*Trachurus symmetricus*), which gather in schools around pilings and kelp beds. Schools are large groups of fish that swim, hunt, defend territory, and even spawn together. A swirling school of silvery fish confuses a predator and makes it difficult for it to single out any one fish. Their highly attuned senses detect tiny movements in each other, so they can twist and maneuver as one mass. Small fish, like the Pacific Jack Mackerel and the Salema, spend almost their entire lives in schools for camouflage and protection. The mackerel is a slender, narrow fish, about 8 inches long with a silvery belly and bluish green stripes or spots along its back. The Salema is about 6 inches long; the golden stripes along its silver back and sides make it one of the flashiest fishes in coastal waters.

It's exciting to watch schools flash by under a pier; unfortunately the so-called peaceful Pacific is often dark and turbulent, so schools of fish are an infrequent sight. To get an idea of the different species of Southern California's nearshore fish, check a local marine aquarium or talk to local fishermen and ask to take a peek at their catches. Many fishermen are happy to share their knowledge with you. Fishing is an important commercial and recreational industry in Southern California. Licensing and fishing regulations try to ensure a healthy balance between the needs of the fishing industry and fish populations. For example, there are restrictions on catching Barred Surfperch because its population has plummeted.

The Barred Surfperch (*Amphistichus argenteus*) gives birth to live young. The eggs are fertilized within the female's body, and she carries them for five to six months. Females gather in shallow, peaceful bays and inlets in spring and early summer and give birth to less than a dozen young per year. This is an extremely low birthrate that could endanger the species if California didn't have stiff fishing restrictions. Look for the Barred Surfperch along sandy beaches where it follows sand crabs up the shore and snatches them from their burrows before the waves retreat. It has silver scales with gray or black vertical bars on its sides.

Salema
(Xenistius
californiensis)

*Pacific Jack
Mackerel*
(Trachurus
symmetricus)
—Phillip Colla/
oceanlight.com

*Barred
Surfperch*
(Amphistichus
argenteus)

California Sheephead (*Semicossyphus pulcher*)

The California Sheephead (*Semicossyphus pulcher*) is a fascinating species that undergoes many changes during the course of its life. It has one of the most interesting life cycles of all the marine species along the Southern California coast. Initially, all California Sheepheads are female. They start life as minute fry and are red with a white stripe and black dots on their fins. As the fry grow in protected reefs and kelp beds, their coloring changes to salmon or pink. At roughly eight years of age, when a California Sheephead can begin to breed, it is around 1 foot long. This is also the age when a remarkable change can occur: if there are no males in the vicinity, some of the females change gender. Gradually, a female will develop testes, which is signaled by the appearance of black bands across the fish's head and tail, a red band across its middle, and a white chin and belly. Eventually its head becomes large, bulbous, and, with some imagination, sheeplike. She, or rather he, can then fertilize eggs laid by the females.

The California Sheephead is common in kelp beds south of Point Conception, where it dines on hard-shelled mollusks and sea urchins. The sheephead's strong teeth easily crush and grind the shells and exoskeletons. Since an overabundance of urchins can destroy kelp holdfasts and potentially uproot the undersea kelp forest, a healthy California Sheephead population is vital to keep urchins in balance. Marine reserves along the coast help maintain and increase populations by creating habitat sanctuaries where fish and other creatures can thrive free of human predation.

California Sheephead (Semicossyphus pulcher) —Phillip Colla/oceanlight.com

Garibaldi (*Hypsypops rubicundus*)

You might see the feisty orange Garibaldi darting among rocks along the shore when the tide is out, but its favorite habitat is the kelp forest. Kelp forests support a lot of the marine life that the Garibaldi dines upon, such as sponges and small algae. In addition, kelp provides the Garibaldi a place to hide from sea lions and other predators.

Unlike most animals, the Garibaldi male raises its young alone. It chooses a nest site along a rock; carefully cleans off most of the plants and animals living there, allowing only certain algae to remain; and entices a female to lay her eggs in the nest. If the nest meets with her approval, she lays her eggs and the male covers them with sperm. The female then moves on—her job in the life cycle completed—and the male maintains the nest in order to attract different females to lay as many eggs as possible. It takes about two weeks for fry to hatch, and the male Garibaldi will fiercely defend his nest the entire time, even fearlessly confronting divers. As the young fish mature, they develop spectacular neon blue spots on their orange scales. This dappled effect camouflages them from predators.

At one time, the Garibaldi was a species marine aquarium hobbyists liked to collect. Overfishing and collecting caused its numbers to drop to an alarming low, and in 1995 it was awarded special status as the California State Marine Fish in order to protect it. There is absolutely no catch allowed, and as a result populations have recovered well, especially south of Point Conception where warmer waters provide the optimal environment for this beautiful creature.

Garibaldi (Hypsypops rubicundus) —Phillip Colla/oceanlight.com

California Scorpionfish (*Scorpaena guttata*)
Treefish (*Sebastes serriceps*)

The California Scorpionfish and the Treefish share some interesting physical traits—most notably the poisonous spines near their fins and the short, nonpoisonous spines on their heads. Although they look very different, they belong to the same order, Scorpaeniformes, which refers to the burning sting their spines can inflict. The spines, however, are only defensive tools to protect these timid creatures, which live in rocky and kelp habitats near the shore.

The California Scorpionfish (*Scorpaena guttata*), which grows up to 1½ feet long, has a broad face and bulging eyes that cause it to have a startled countenance. It is a sedentary fish, hiding among rocks and sometimes just lying in wait for smaller fish, shrimp, and other small crustaceans to swim into its mouth. Prey will do this since the California Scorpionfish is well camouflaged with reddish brown spots.

The 1½-foot-long Treefish (*Sebastes serriceps*) is a member of the large *Sebastes* genus, which includes at least fifty species in Southern California. Species of *Sebastes* are collectively known as *rockfish* because they live on rocky substrates. They are sold on the fish market as *rock cod* or *Pacific red snapper*. In addition, the Treefish is sometimes called the *Convict Fish* because of its broad, dark stripes, which make the fish look like it's wearing an old-fashioned prison uniform.

Rockfish have extremely long lives—well over one hundred years—and very low reproductive rates. Most are *ovoviviparous,* which means they bear live young, like the Barred Surfperch (*Amphistichus argenteus*). This adaptation offers fish larvae increased protection during developmental stages, but it also means rockfish have far fewer offspring than egg-laying species. Rockfish grow very slowly, and they may not breed until they are at least ten years old. Because they are also very tasty, there has been a high demand for them in restaurants and fish markets, and overfishing has resulted in a sharp and alarming decline in their numbers. Moratoriums on fishing, catch restrictions, and habitat reserves are three strategies that Southern California officials believe will help increase the rockfish population.

California Scorpionfish (Scorpaena guttata) *photographed in Heal the Bay's Santa Monica Pier Aquarium*

Treefish (Sebastes serriceps)

California Moray Eel (*Gymnothorax mordax*)

Because it lurks in dark crevices and has eyes that seem to stare madly ahead, a mouth that slowly opens and closes revealing sharp teeth, and a snakelike body, people tend to fear the California Moray Eel (*Gymnothorax mordax*) like the Big Bad Wolf. Unfortunately, the moray eel has an image problem. It actually is a shy creature that would much rather flee danger than confront it.

Admittedly, the moray does look formidable, but there are reasons for its behavior and appearance that have nothing to do with the fear it can arouse in us. This eel lurks in dark crevices to protect its soft, scaleless body from predators such as sea lions and dolphins. All fish have eyes that seem to stare because they don't have eyelids or eyelashes and do not blink. What makes the California Moray Eel look more alarming is that it is one of the few fish with eyes that face nearly forward. This gives onlookers the impression that the eel is challenging them, when in fact it is probably looking for an escape route. Its mouth opens and closes because eels don't have external gill slits, so the movement of the mouth pumps water into the eel's body, allowing it to breathe. And finally, the eel's snakelike body is an excellent adaptation to life among the rocks, enabling it to fit into narrow crevices where it can safely find food.

That said, the California Moray Eel can give a bad bite if backed into a corner with no way to escape. It has strong jaws and teeth designed to hold on to its dinner, such as octopuses and fish. Even so, it is a misunderstood creature with a bad reputation based on superficial impressions. Morays can grow up to 5 feet long; their bodies are gray with yellow and brown speckles that help camouflage them. At times of extreme low tides (minus 1½ feet or so), you may spot a California Moray Eel near a tidepool, usually gliding away toward deeper water. You are more likely to see one while scuba diving or visiting a marine center.

California Moray Eel (Gymnothorax mordax)

CARTILAGINOUS FISH (RAYS AND SHARKS)

Guitarfish (*Rhinobatos productus*)
Thornback Ray (*Platyrhinoidis triseriata*)

The guitar-shaped Guitarfish (*Rhinobatos productus*) is one of the many strange creatures you share the water with if you go for a swim off a sandy beach in Southern California. This shallow-water species is closely related to rays and sharks. Don't worry, though, the Guitarfish has small teeth and does not have a stinger. It's a shy creature that flutters up from the sand and swims off when disturbed; like most sea creatures, it merely wants to be left in peace.

Guitarfish hang out in sandy bays in spring and summer to mate and bear young. Females are ovoviviparous, retaining eggs inside their bodies for about a year while they develop. When born, the pups are about the size of a hand. They grow 4 to 5 feet long. Some marine centers keep Guitarfish in touch tanks or aquariums. They are not particularly slimy; in fact, their smooth gray skin feels like buttery soft leather.

The Thornback Ray (*Platyrhinoidis triseriata*) grows up to 2 feet long; its upper (dorsal) side is dark gray, and its underside (ventral) is white. Like the Guitarfish, it is ovoviviparous. Anglers frequently catch Thornback Rays off fishing piers. This ray is a fierce-looking creature: it is disk shaped like a stingray, has a long thick tail like a Guitarfish, and has three rows of nonpoisonous hooked thorns along its back and tail. Wise anglers use thick gloves to carefully release rays from their fishing lines before throwing them back into the sea.

Like sharks, Guitarfish and Thornback Rays have very flexible bodies because their bones are made of cartilage, the same substance that gives form to our nose and ears. Unlike sharks, which have gill slits on their sides, the gill slits of these species are on the underside of their bodies. These animals eat creatures that live on the ocean floor, such as sand crabs, other small crustaceans, worms, and bivalves. Small holes, or *spiracles,* behind the eyes enable them to breathe while they rest on the seafloor.

Guitarfish (Rhinobatos productus)

Thornback Ray (Platyrhinoidis triseriata)

Round Stingray (*Urobatis halleri*)
Bat Ray (*Myliobatis californicus*)

The Round Stingray and Bay Ray are common inhabitants of shallow coastal waters, and they are why it is important for swimmers and waders to do the "stingray shuffle" along sandy beaches: shuffle your feet as you enter the water in order to stir up sand and creatures ahead of you. A ray has a poisonous barb on its long tail that protects it from predators. Rays are not aggressive creatures, and the barb is only for defensive measures. In fact, people have observed both the Bat Ray and Round Stingray close to unwary waders, and neither animal acted threatening in any way. If stepped on, however, rays reflexively lash their tails. It's their only defense, other than camouflage, since their teeth are small and they are slow swimmers. In the event you are stung, immerse the stung area in very hot water for twenty minutes or more, and seek medical attention if you are among the few people who have an allergic reaction.

The Round Stingray (*Urobatis halleri*) is shaped and colored like a 12-inch pancake. Like all rays, its mouth is a small opening on the underside of its body, and it eats by suctioning small prey—worms, sand crabs, and bivalves—from the sand. Like other rays, it is ovoviviparous.

Known for its graceful, undulating swimming style, the Bat Ray (*Myliobatis californicus*) glides through the water by flapping its huge winglike fins, which can grow up to 6 feet across. It is a gentle, curious creature with large eyes, a box-shaped head, and an underslung snout that curves in such a way that the Bat Ray looks like it's smiling. The snout enables it to scoop up sand or mud for its food, but the Bat Ray's real mouth is a small, flat rectangle on its underside. The mouth contains a lot of little grinding teeth that chomp through mollusks and other hard-shelled creatures. With stingers removed, Bat Rays are popular creatures in touch tanks at marine centers, at least in part because they seem as interested in us as we are in them. They often swim up to visitors and allow the visitors to stroke them.

Round Stingray
(Urobatis halleri)

Bat Ray
(Myliobatis
californicus)

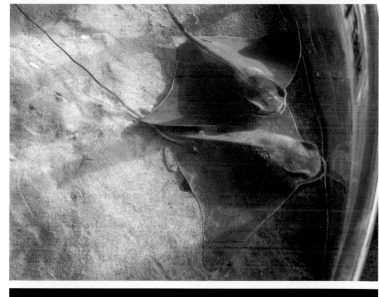

*Underside
of a Bat Ray*

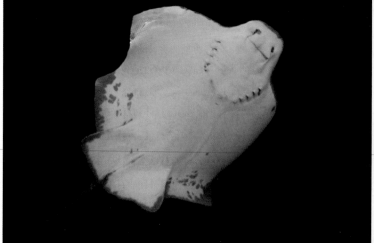

Horn Shark (*Heterodontus francisci*)

Sharks have an unbelievably bad reputation; from the movie *Jaws* to numerous tall tales, many people view sharks as terrifying predators lurking in the deep, just waiting for the chance to maim or eat a human. Nothing could be further from the truth. While there are very large, intimidating sharks off the coast, such as the Great White (*Carcharodon carcharias*), they are hunting large fish, other sharks, seals, and sea lions—not people. Fear of them is out of proportion to the threat sharks actually pose, and unfortunately, people have adverse reactions to even the small, harmless species along the Southern California coast.

The gray, 4-foot-long Horn Shark (*Heterodontus francisci*) is the shark people most commonly see along the Southern California coast. There are many anecdotes about human and Horn Shark interactions that attest to the harmlessness of this species. One of these stories holds that two children found a Horn Shark in a low tidepool. Thinking it was a baby sperm whale because of its gray color and blunt head, they decided they had better "rescue" the stranded creature. One can only wonder what the Horn Shark though of this, but no harm was done, and it swam peaceably away.

The Horn Shark is named for the two sharp horns that project from the dorsal fins along its back, which are a nasty mouthful for would-be predators. The Horn Shark lives in nearshore waters, hiding among rocks during the day and feeding on mollusks, fish, and crustaceans at night. Although many sharks give birth to live young, and some even nourish them with structures like a placenta and umbilical cord, the Horn Shark lays amazing spiral-shaped eggs that are about 3 inches long and contain one embryo. The corkscrew design helps anchor them between rocks.

Sharks have remained much the same for the past 100 million years. They are adapted to thrive in the ocean. One secret of their success is their skin, which is made of *dermal denticles*—small scalelike teeth that act as a suit of armor and make their bodies more hydrodynamic. Stroked from head to tail, a shark feels smooth; if you stroke one from tail to head, though, the skin is rough enough to inflict a nasty scrape. The Chumash and Tongva tribes used sharkskin as sandpaper.

Horn Shark (Heterodontus francisci) —Phillip Colla/oceanlight.com

Horn Shark egg

Swell Shark (*Cephaloscyllium ventriosum*)
Leopard Shark (*Triakis semifasciata*)

The Swell Shark's (*Cephaloscyllium ventriosum*) brown, gray, and yellow mottled coloring and relatively small size (about 3 feet long) camouflages it from predators. Unlike typical sharks, the Swell Shark has a smooth back and only a small dorsal fin near its tail. This sleek design enables it to fit more easily in rock crevices. At night, it glides along the sandy ocean floor searching for invertebrates and small fish, but when danger looms, the Swell Shark abandons its svelte profile. It takes a huge gulp of water and swells up like a balloon, wedging itself tightly into crevices. It becomes as difficult to bite as a basketball! Confronted with a shark that has suddenly doubled its size, taken on the shape of a balloon, and is very difficult to get at, most predators give up.

You might find the Swell Shark's egg casing, or *mermaid's purse,* while exploring a kelp wrack. It's a tough, 3-inch-long, brownish rectangle with curling strings on each corner. These tendrils tangle the casing in kelp or snag it on a rock, keeping the egg casing from drifting during the nine months or so that it takes for a baby shark to develop. Like all fish, sharks are fully functional when they hatch so they can survive; but sharks are complex creatures, so their gestation period is longer. Water temperatures can also affect how long the shark's gestation period lasts.

Like most sharks, the mother Leopard Shark (*Triakis semifasciata*) retains fertilized eggs in her body and gives birth to live young. Leopard Sharks are elusive and shy creatures, but anglers regularly catch them in shallow waters that have sandy or muddy bottoms, where the sharks feed on clam siphons, other invertebrates, and small fish. The Leopard Shark is slender, about 6 feet long, has a graceful, sinuous swimming style, and has a dappled and striped body that perfectly camouflages it in waters past the surf zone. Most fish have *swim bladders,* a pouchlike organ filled with air that helps keep them buoyant. A shark, however, does not have a swim bladder; instead it has an oil-filled liver that keeps it buoyant.

A just-hatched Swell Shark (Cephaloscyllium ventriosum)

Swell Shark mermaid's purse

Leopard Shark (Triakis semifasciata)

Marine Mammals
SEA LIONS

California Sea Lion (*Zalophus californianus*)

The California Sea Lion (*Zalophus californianus*) is one of the most beloved marine animals, and it is instantly familiar to anyone who has ever seen a trained "seal" balancing a ball on its nose. These mammals are intelligent and playful, and zoos and aquariums around the world use this pinniped for entertainment and educational programs more than any other marine animal.

You might see California Sea Lions drifting on the sea with their flippers in the air, which act as solar panels, helping them stay warm; cavorting through harbor waters; or resting on buoys, their loud barks echoing over rocks and waves. Considering their size, sea lions are amazingly graceful in water. They can twist and turn like tornadoes, and they can dive over 100 feet and remain submerged for almost ten minutes as they hunt fish, squid, crustaceans, and small sharks. The adult male sea lion can reach 800 pounds and is four times heavier than the female, though they both grow to about 6 feet long. You can also identify an adult male by the large bumplike protrusion on its forehead. This is called a *sagittal crest*.

Most often seen on buoys and breakwater rocks, sea lions also haul out onto beaches and rocks all along the Pacific coast. The Channel Islands are the California Sea Lion's breeding grounds in Southern California. Males arrive from their northern feeding grounds in May to establish territories and harems. After mating, the males migrate north again, at least as far as Año Nuevo State Reserve near San Francisco and sometimes even up into the nutrient-rich waters of British Columbia. The gestation period for this animal is about one year. Females give birth and raise their pups on the Channel Islands, and when they are old enough to swim, the pups follow the mothers into nearshore waters.

Pups stay with their mothers until they are weaned, up to a year. You might see pups parked along rocks from Santa Barbara to Coronado while their mothers hunt unseen in the water. Some people become concerned when they see this, wondering if the pup has been abandoned. The beach is part of the sea lion's natural habitat, though, and pups remaining unattended for even a day or two is completely normal. The babies have stores of fat to nourish them when their mothers are away feeding.

Sea lions can lift their bodies on all four flippers and walk, lunge, and run faster than people imagine; and of course, they can bite in self-defense. Although they are adorable, please remember that sea lions are wild animals and you should not approach them. Stay at least 50 feet away for your own safety.

California Sea Lions (Zalophus californianus); *male on far left*

A baby (back) *and adult female* (front) *California Sea Lion*

SEALS

Harbor Seal (*Phoca vitulina*)

There is something almost feline about seals—lolling on rocks or sand, they look like fat, self-satisfied cats. Their beautiful almond-shaped eyes and flat face add to this impression, and like a cat, the seal is not as sociable or trainable as the sea lion, which is more doglike in its appearance and personality.

Many people confuse seals with sea lions, but look closely: All four of the sea lion's limbs are long flippers; seals have back flippers, but the front ones are smaller and pawlike. Sea lions are solid brown or grey; seals are usually dotted, spotted, or mottled, and range in color from silver to black. Sea lions have tiny ear flaps; a seal's ears are flat, round openings that are mostly obscured by fur. Sea lions have pointed, dog-like muzzles; seals have rounder, flatter faces. Sea lions bark; seals are silent except for the occasional grunt and growl. Sea lions can walk on all four flippers; seals scoot on their bellies. Both species are pinnipeds, which, roughly translated from Latin, means "winged foot." Although extremely clumsy on land, underwater these creatures seem winged indeed. They are graceful and glorious swimmers.

Harbor Seals (*Phoca vitulina*) are not as common as sea lions, and they are very wary creatures. Loud noises, even the soft click of a camera shutter, can easily startle them. There are several haul-out sites where they feel safe enough to spend time out of water in Southern California, such as Casa Beach in La Jolla and Carpinteria State Beach in Santa Barbara County; the latter is their only mainland pupping site—where they birth their young. Harbor Seals have a ten-month gestation period, and they nurse their young for about a month, during which time the pup can double its birth weight. After the pup is weaned, it separates from its mother and goes off on its own. Like sea lions, Harbor Seals mostly eat fish. Large sharks may prey on them.

It is a treat to stand on a wall or cliff above them and watch them relax in the sun. They twist and stretch their bodies in circles and back bends, wash their faces or gnaw on their paws like cats, and curl and uncurl their back flippers as though they are wiggling their toes with delight.

Harbor Seal
(Phoca vitulina)

Harbor Seals

Harbor Seal

DOLPHINS

Common Dolphin (*Delphinus* species)
Bottlenose Dolphin (*Tursiops truncatus*)
Risso's Dolphin (*Grampus griseus*)
Pacific White-Sided Dolphin (*Lagenorhynchus obliquidens*)

Beloved throughout human history, the dolphin's playfulness and intelligence has made it one of the most intriguing animals in the world. Cultural legends abound about its role as a benefactor, beginning with an ancient Greek myth: the story holds that a dolphin helped Poseidon, the Greek god of the sea, find a bride up the inlets of Delphi. The Common Dolphin's name, *Delphinus,* is derived from this story. Some ancient peoples believed that dolphins guided people across the River Styx, and that dolphins were actually drowning sailors who had been transformed. Perhaps these stories helped people explain why wild dolphins seemed to take pity on people who were in distress in the water. There are documented cases of dolphins towing people to safety. In Christianity, dolphins have been used to symbolize conversion and inner peace. It is easy to believe, as the Chumash Indians did, that the dolphin is a brother and kindred spirit.

Dolphins are members of the cetacean order, a collection of warm-blooded mammals that includes whales with baleen teeth, like the Gray Whale (*Eschrictius robustus*), as well as toothed whales, such as dolphins, porpoises, Killer Whales (*Orcinus orca*), and Sperm Whales (*Physeter macrocephalus*). Every cetacean breathes through a blowhole on top of its head. They give birth to live young, which they nurse by squirting milk through the water to their babies. Cetaceans have a gestation period of approximately a year and give birth to one calf—rarely twins. They care for their young, even lifting newborns to the surface until they can breathe on their own.

We seem to have an innate response to the joyousness that dolphins embody. Traffic will come to a standstill along the coast as people stop their cars to watch dolphins playing in the surf. Generally, dolphins are more playful than whales, and frequently they leap clear of the water, sometimes in unison, when they race. When swimming at top speed, dolphins can breathe more quickly and easily by leaping clear of the water. Dolphins also frequently *bow ride*—speed to the front of a boat and let its forward wave "push" them through the water. It is very exciting to speed through the water while dolphins jostle for position and leap over each other on all sides of the boat. Researchers have not discovered a biological reason for bow riding, and this has led many of them to conclude that dolphins merely like to race through the water.

Common Dolphin
(length: 5–6 feet)

Pacific
White-Sided
Dolphin
(length: 6–7 feet)

Bottlenose
Dolphin
(length: 8–10 feet)

Risso's Dolphin
(length: 14 feet)

Chart of dolphin shapes and sizes

Body language and vocalizations are two ways that dolphins communicate and keep track of each other. Although it can be playful at times, body language can also convey aggression, such as when they lift their tails out of the water and slap the water's surface—called *lobtailing*. Dolphins also communicate through squeals, squeaks, and whistles. Like seals, mothers appear to have a special voice or sound they use as they nurture and teach their young. Marine scientists speculate that this special sound is a name that identifies an individual within the pod and helps to bond the group. Dolphins work together to protect and care for their pod, fending off shark attacks, hunting cooperatively, and helping ill or injured dolphins to the surface to breathe.

Their socializing sounds appear to be a language separate from the echolocation they use to locate prey. Dolphins identify the size, shape, and distance of creatures and objects in the water by emitting high-pitched sounds and listening to the echoes that return. This ability is not infallible, and sometimes dolphins consume garbage that mimics the shape of natural prey. Plastic bags, for example, appear much like jellies to a dolphin, while a shredded balloon may look like a fish, squid, or octopus. Sadly, dolphins are maimed and killed by plastic and other garbage that people throw from boats or that is washed into the ocean from storm drains.

Dolphin species are difficult to distinguish because we seldom get more than a glimpse of their bodies as they surface or leap. Different species of the Common Dolphin, also known as the *Saddleback Dolphin,* are distributed worldwide, and it is the dolphin people most commonly spot in Southern California waters. They are highly social animals and travel in pods of up to several thousand individuals, but close to shore they usually travel in smaller groups. There are two species that occur in Southern California: the Short-Beaked Dolphin (*Delphinus delphis*) and the Long-Beaked Dolphin (*Delphinus capensis*). Both of them are small—5 to 7 feet long—and have dark backs and a crisscross pattern of yellow and grey bands along their sides.

There are many stories of Common Dolphins interacting with humans and even staying in contact with them, apparently as a substitute for the dolphin's pod. However, Common Dolphins do poorly in captivity, unlike the Bottlenose Dolphin (*Tursiops truncatus*), made famous by the TV program *Flipper* and countless aquarium shows. Like all dolphins, the bottlenose is highly intelligent, and it is also more adaptable to human contact than the Common Dolphin. As a result, people have used the Bottlenose Dolphin for entertainment, education, and research to better understand dolphin language and behavior. Even

Bottlenose Dolphin
(Tursiops truncatus)
—U.S. Navy Marine
Mammal Program

*A Bottlenose
Dolphin taking
its first breath*
—U.S. Navy
Marine Mammal
Program

the navy has used this dolphin to retrieve or identify dangerous objects, much like a specially trained police dog.

You can easily identify a Risso's Dolphin (*Grampus griseus*) by its large size, blunt head, and tall dorsal fin. Depending on how sunny the day is, dolphins can appear light tan or light gray; the Risso's Dolphin is unmistakable with its pale skin and even paler mottling of scars. This buildup of noticeable scars, caused by fights, mating, and play, is unique to this species. The Risso's Dolphin swims noticeably slower than other dolphins and cruises at the water's surface. You'll be able to see its large dorsal fin slicing through the water for long distances. Other dolphin species surface briefly, and you will only get intermittent glimpses of their dorsal fins as they curve through the water. The Risso's Dolphin lives in nearshore waters year-round. The Pacific White-Sided Dolphin (*Lagenorhynchus obliquidens*), on the other hand, spends most of the year far out to sea, coming closer to shore only in winter; you can identify it by its black-and-white dorsal fin.

Common Dolphin
(Delphinus
species)
—Phillip Colla/
oceanlight.com

Risso's Dolphin
(Grampus
griseus)

*Pacific White-
Sided Dolphin*
(Lagenorhynchus
obliquidens)
—Phillip Colla/
oceanlight.com

GRAY WHALE

Gray Whale (*Eschrichtius robustus*)

Each year, magnificent Gray Whales (*Eschrichtius robustus*) migrate along the Pacific coast from the Bering Strait in Alaska to lagoons in Baja California, Mexico, where they rest, breed, and give birth to young before returning north again—a total of 12,500 miles a year. They pass Point Conception in late December, coming south, and are visible in Southern California waters until about May, when the last of the mothers and babies pass by on their journey north. However, during the summer, special tours can be found that travel out to the Channel Islands to view the increasing numbers of Blue Whales (*Balaenoptera musculus*) and Humpback Whales (*Megaptera novaeangliae*)—rare sights in Southern California—that are attracted to the krill in that area.

You can view the Gray Whale migration from cliffs that project out over the Pacific, long fishing piers, and even from beaches. The mothers have been known to hug the shoreline just a few hundred yards off beaches in midspring, escorting their babies north. The most successful way to view Gray Whales is on a whale-watching trip. You might see a Gray Whale nudging her curious calf away from a boat, babies playing, what looks like a crusty gray island surfacing alongside the boat, or a pod of whales spouting in the distance or lifting their flukes (tail flipper) out of the water.

Gray Whales grow up to 45 feet long and can weigh close to 75,000 pounds. Unlike toothed whales that have one blowhole, a Gray Whale breathes through two holes at the top of its head. These whales produce a noticeable spout, or blow, that looks like a heart-shaped puff of steam. Experts can tell whale species apart by the shape of their blow. A unique species of barnacle (*Cryptolepas rhachianecti*), found only on Gray Whales, forms crusty white patches on the skin of these whales. In place of a dorsal fin, a Gray Whale has a distinctive, bumpy *knuckle-ridge* that runs down its back to its tail.

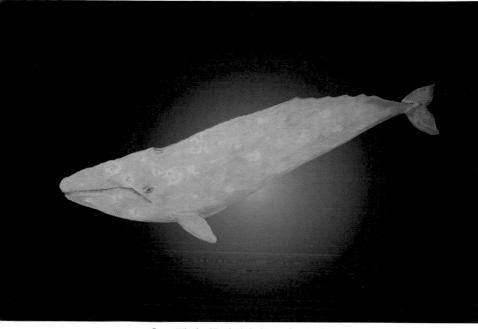

Gray Whale (Eschrichtius robustus)

Gray Whales behind Catalina Island

Like a dolphin, a Gray Whale sometimes breaches—it lifts part of its immense body out of the water and then lands on its side with a huge splash. When this happens, all activity on a nearby beach or boat comes to a standstill as people gaze like spectators at a fireworks display. Although some researchers think that perhaps the whale is merely trying to knock parasites off its skin, no one really knows for sure why whales breach. Whales also *sky hop,* or *spy hop.* Unlike breaching, when a whale sky hops it does not leap; it merely stands vertically with its head out of the water to the level of the whale's eyes. Again, there are theories about this behavior. Some researchers believe the whale is looking at the land to get its bearings, but no one knows for sure.

Instead of teeth, a Gray Whale has *baleen plates,* which are thin brushy fibers made of keratin—the same protein hair and fingernails are made of. Baleen grows from the roof of the whale's mouth, and the whale eats by scraping the side of its mouth along the ocean floor and scooping up mud and water. Scientists can tell whether a whale is right- or left-handed by determining which side of its mouth has fewer skin parasites; the side with fewer parasites and worn baleen is the side that scrapes the bottom—the side the whale favors. The catch is strained through the baleen, which captures all sorts of small invertebrates. It is fascinating that minute creatures can sustain a gigantic whale. Besides humans, the Gray Whale has no predators, though Great White Sharks and Killer Whales will attack calves.

Whales and dolphins have flukes that are oriented along the horizontal plane of their bodies. Flukes are the lobes on their tails, and they give these mammals an undulating, up-and-down movement as they swim. All fish, on the other hand, have vertical tails, and a fish swims by wriggling side to side. Just before a whale dives, it may lift its flukes out of the water. Once you see that—unless the whale is slapping the surface of the water to communicate with other whales—the whale may stay underwater for up to twenty minutes and come up ½ mile away, so the fluke sighting seems like the whale's way of waving good-bye.

A Gray Whale (Eschrichtius robustus) *in the Bering Strait*
—Photo courtesy of NOAA Office of Corps Operations

Gray Whale flukes

Birds

Observing birds in their environment is one of the most rewarding activities while visiting the beach. Many people are not aware of how vital our shores and wetlands are to birds—and how fragile these habitats have become. In undeveloped coastal habitats, where rivers or creeks empty into the ocean, mudflats, salt marshes, and estuaries develop. But in Southern California, most of these areas are covered with buildings or have been turned into marinas and harbors. In urban centers, such as Los Angeles, rivers and creeks have been lined with concrete to form flood-control channels that direct street runoff into the ocean. In fact, less than 10 percent of Southern California's original coastal wetlands survives—a loss comparable to the loss of rain forest in a third world country.

Southern California's remaining coastal wetlands are among the most valuable habitats in the world. They harbor many forms of wildlife, from invertebrates to mammals, are nurseries for fishes and rays, and provide essential habitat for migratory birds. When you visit these areas you can see that even after one hundred years of human development, we have not completely altered the patterns and habits that wildlife have developed over millennia. California lies under the Pacific Fly Zone, a major migratory bird route in North America. Although many species head north to their nesting areas in summer, from September through May the Southern California coast is a bird-watcher's paradise. Birds come to find warmth, a resting place, and feeding grounds. They are an important part of the complex food web, helping keep nature in balance.

I start this section with common seashore birds and then profile representative coastal wetland species, including a few endangered species. I include information on bird behavior, habitats where you are likely to encounter a species, and physical descriptions. The plumage of inland birds is often gender specific—males are brightly colored, females are drab. However, this is not the case for most North American coastal birds. Both sexes look alike in breeding and nonbreeding plumage, and the variation between juveniles and adults is subtle. When there

Urban buildup results in a loss of dune and wetland areas.

Bird-watchers at Bolsa Chica Ecological Reserve, a wetland reclaimed from oil fields in Orange County

are major differences in plumage because of gender and age, I note that. I also give approximate body lengths of adult birds.

Please remember that you should never feed birds, and you should leave dogs at home when visiting the beach. In designated wetlands, you should stay on marked paths or trails to minimize the impact on fragile feeding or nesting areas.

A Western Gull (Larus occidentalis) *rests on a rock*

Nearshore Birds

GULLS

Gulls squabbling over a french fry in the beach parking lot hardly seem like majestic creatures. However, watch as they soar overhead, float peacefully on the waves, hunker down in the sand, or stalk along the beach. They are beautiful animals. As gulls are among the largest and tamest of wild birds, it is very rewarding to watch them. They are the bold pirates of the shore, and they live in all beach environments.

With all the natural food on the beach, it is amazing that gulls will overturn picnic baskets, pick through snacks, and even try to drink out of an open can of soda. Their raucous cries announce to every gull on the beach that there is food up for grabs. Gulls aren't deterred a bit by a cloth or beach towel covering food. They'll snatch it off and drag away a whole picnic. Picnickers must anchor a cover with rocks or other heavy items, or they can expect to come back from a stroll to find nothing left.

Though annoying, a gull's curiosity and opportunistic behavior are gifts that enable it to adapt and thrive in many different environments. Gulls are nature's scavengers, and they typically hang out around fishermen. If begging doesn't work, they will try to steal fish right off the line, sometimes getting punctured by the fishhook or strangled by the fishing line. Sometimes gulls consume garbage or get entangled in plastic, which maims or kills them.

Gulls will also probe for bean clams and sand crabs, just like sandpipers, and pick snails off exposed rocks or pilings. To get at the meat of bivalves, gulls have been known to drop pebbles on them, or they carry the mollusks high into the air and drop them on rocks to crack their shells. A gull will follow a pelican as it dives for fish and then steal the pelican's catch. Gulls also search through newly washed-up wracks of kelp for eggs, small shellfish, and crabs. The quickest way to determine if a wrack is worth exploring is to note whether or not gulls are paying special attention to it or are guarding it with more than usual vigor. Perched atop a wrack, a gull may announce his primacy with loud screams. Barking, squealing, murmured growls, and trumpetlike calls are just a few of the ways these birds communicate with each other.

Although these birds are highly competitive, you may witness quiet interactions. For example, courting gulls circle each other with elaborate bows and head bobbing and even walk in tandem for a few steps. A young gull will sometimes beg, with head lowered, for a scrap

This gull was caught in a fishing line but soared away uninjured after the fisherman released it.

Western Gull (Larus occidentalis)

A Western Gull investigates.

of food from another gull. Usually the other bird ignores it, but a little food sharing may indicate a parent and child relationship. All of these behaviors are fun to witness.

Herring Gull (*Larus argentatus*)
Glaucous-Winged Gull (*Larus glaucescens*)
California Gull (*Larus californicus*)
Western Gull (*Larus occidentalis*)

Because all seabirds are mobile, they can be found in almost any coastal environment. However, the "seashore"—the relatively narrow strip between the beach and the swelling breakers—is a highway for gulls, terns, pelicans, and cormorants. Cormorants float and dive on nearshore waters, while terns gaze down on the water as they soar, and pelicans glide between the breakers. Each of these species also rests on the sand or rocks near the water, where you may get to see them up close.

Large gulls have a lot in common: they are noisy and aggressive, have wingspans of more than 4 feet, and have mottled gray and brown feathers for three or four years as they gradually develop adult plumage. Since they look so much alike, it can be a challenge to identify a gull's species, especially in winter when Herring Gulls (*Larus argentatus*), Glaucous-Winged Gulls (*Larus glaucescens*), and California Gulls (*Larus californicus*) Gulls visit Southern California. However, there are a couple of details to look for: Herring Gulls retain mottled brown neck feathers as adults and have light gray wings with black wing tips; the Glaucous-Winged Gull has gray wing tips and overall is much paler. When in flight, it looks like it is all white. Juveniles have bills that are completely black and, overall, pale tan mottled feathers.

The California Gull, the state bird of Utah, visits the coast for part of winter. It can easily be identified because it has a black smudge overlaying the red dot on its bill, and it is the only large gull common to Southern California that has yellow legs—a fitting color for a bird named after the Golden State.

In summer, gull identification is a cinch because the Western Gull (*Larus occidentalis*) is the only large gull in Southern California. In fact, this gull is the most common gull on the coast. Other than a couple of months in spring when the adults have moved to their breeding grounds, it occurs in every beach habitat. The Western Gull and California Gull are the two gulls that look most similar, but the Western Gull is slightly larger. And when it is fully mature, it doesn't have a black ring next to the red dot on its bill. To accurately identify the Western Gull, though, look for charcoal gray wings, yellow eyes, and pink legs.

Herring Gull
(Larus argentatus)

Western Gull
(Larus occidentalis)

A juvenile Glaucous-Winged Gull
(Larus glaucescens)

California Gull
(Larus californicus)

Heerman's Gull (*Larus heermanni*)
Ring-Billed Gull (*Larus delawarensis*)
Bonaparte's Gull (*Larus philadelphia*)

The Heerman's Gull, Ring-Billed Gull, and Bonaparte's Gull are the *Vogue* models of small- to medium-sized gulls along the Southern California coast. Each gull is elegantly color coordinated with matching eye ring and bill colors.

The Heerman's Gull (*Larus heermanni*) is about 20 inches long and is the easiest to identify because it is the only adult gull with a gray breast. The juvenile is completely dark brown or sooty colored, including its legs and the tip of its bill. As it matures, its bill turns bright lipstick red, its brown plumage becomes soft gray, and during breeding season its head is white. This gull's eyes are circled by a thin ring of jewel-like red flesh that matches its red bill. The Heerman's Gull has a low-pitched call, and when it begs it makes a distinctive doglike barking sound.

The adult Ring-Billed Gull (*Larus delawarensis*) is smallish, about 16 inches long, with bright yellow legs, a matching bill with a black ring, and beautiful yellow eyes rimmed with a ruby red eye ring. Occasionally people mistake it for the California Gull (*Larus californicus*), but the Ring-Billed Gull is paler, much smaller, has a smaller bill, and can be found in Southern California year-round.

The Bonaparte's Gull (*Larus philadelphia*) is the smallest gull that commonly visits Southern California. Only slightly larger than a pigeon, it seems to have a less aggressive personality than the other gulls. It has a small black bill, and during breeding season it has a black head. People usually see this bird in Southern California in winter, though, when its head plumage is white and it has a black spot behind its eye. It likes quiet bays and salt marshes, where you may see it picking fish from the surface of the water.

Gulls and terns look a lot alike, but tern wings are narrow, pointed, and more streamlined than the wings of gulls. Because of this, terns can hover gracefully, while gulls cannot. This doesn't stop gulls from attempting to hover, though. If a gull spots food while soaring, it will try to hover above it, but it seems to be a real struggle. It can only hover for a second or two, and only with a lot of awkward flapping, tail wagging, and foot spreading—it's very comical.

Adult Heerman's Gull (Larus heermanni)

Ring-Billed Gull (Larus delawarensis)

Bonaparte's Gull (Larus philadelphia) *in winter plumage*

TERNS

Caspian Tern (*Sterna caspia*)
Elegant Tern (*Sterna elegans*)

Rocketing overhead or hunkered down on the sand, terns are beautiful, graceful, and intriguing birds. Every year terns migrate thousands of miles from northern regions to Latin America and back north again. Along their journey they visit Southern California shores to feed, breed, and rest.

Superficially, terns are similar to gulls, but there are behaviors and physical characteristics that distinguish them. For example, gulls rarely hover. This is an awkward move for them, so if you see what looks like a gull levitating over the surf with quivering wings, be assured that it is a tern. Terns are expert divers; when a tern spots its prey, it plunges headfirst into the water and comes up in a shimmer of wings, usually with a silvery fish clamped in its bill. Terns have narrow, pointed wings, enabling them to fly faster and maneuver more swiftly than gulls. Also, a tern has a forked tail, unlike a gull, and when a tern hunts, it tends to carry its head at a right angle to its body, looking straight down into the water from high above. Terns often stand on sandbars in estuaries, but they seldom land on water because their relatively small legs make them poor swimmers; gulls do swim. On a harbor cruise you may see terns floating atop kelp.

Caspian (*Sterna caspia*) and Royal (*Sterna maxima*) Terns are about 20 inches long and have wingspans of nearly 4 feet—almost as wide as the wingspans of the largest gulls. The Royal Tern visits Southern California from winter into spring; the Caspian Tern is a year-round resident. In spring, these two species are virtually indistinguishable with their black caps and bright red bills, but the Caspian Tern is somewhat larger than the Royal Tern, and its call is a frequent and unmistakable croaking scream. The Royal Tern's call is a rolling gargle or growling sound.

The Elegant Tern (*Sterna elegans*) is slightly smaller than the other two and has a head plume that is more airy; it ruffles in the wind and the bird can raise and lower it to communicate with its flock. Its bill shades from peach to rose colored and curves down at the end. The Elegant Tern also has pale pink neck feathers, though from a distance the neck looks white. In April and May, Elegant Terns gather in flocks on sandy beaches and coastal wetlands to engage in elaborate court-ship displays that include head bobbing, tandem walking, and plume ruffling. Then pairs will take to the sky to soar and dive toward each other, moving through the sky like rockets.

Caspian Tern
(Sterna caspia)

Center left:
Caspian Tern
flying —Lee Karney
photo, U.S. Fish and
Wildlife Service

Center right:
Terns

Flock of Elegant
Terns (Sterna
elegans)

Forster's Tern (*Sterna forsteri*)
Least Tern (*Sterna antillarum*)

The Forster's Tern (*Sterna forsteri*) is about 1 foot long and is the most common small tern in Southern California. It is a resident year-round. It has a red bill with a black tip and small red legs, and like all terns its legs look too small for its body. Juvenile birds look like adults, but they have rusty colored stripes across their shoulders. In winter, the Forster's Tern has a white head that is bordered by a fringe of black feathers around its eyes. With this plumage, it looks a bit like a bald and frowning cranky old man when hunkered down on the sand on a cold winter day. However, in summer its cap turns black—very stylish!

The Least Tern (*Sterna antillarum*) is the smallest tern in Southern California. It is a mere 9 inches long and the only tern with a yellow bill; juveniles have black bills. Sadly, the Least Tern is an endangered species. It used to breed all along the dunes and sandy estuaries of Southern California, where creeks and rivers empty into the ocean, but the loss of habitat and massive amount of human traffic and activity along the coast have had a huge impact on the Least Tern population.

Terns build nests with just a few twigs on the warm sand and are colonial nesters, which means they nest among other birds. Colonies operate as early warning systems, making it more difficult for predators to target any one particular nest or fledgling. Gulls and crows are indigenous predators of young Least Terns, but Least Terns must also contend with cats and dogs. It is illegal to have an unleashed pet in a dune area on most beaches, but not everyone knows or cares about the plight of these birds and their shrinking habitat.

Local environmentalists, bird watchers, and nature lovers, as well as city, state, and federal authorities, are working to reestablish safe nesting sites for the Least Tern—fencing in their nesting areas, setting up scarecrows to keep crows at bay, and diligently checking for nesting success. The best place to see one of these feisty flyers is above shallow coastal waters, or at a coastal wetland.

Forster's Tern (Sterna forsteri)

Least Tern (Sterna antillarum) —S. Maslowski photo, U.S. Fish and Wildlife Service

SKIMMER

Black Skimmer (*Rynchops niger*)

The Black Skimmer (*Rynchops niger*) is a relative newcomer to Southern California. Migrating north from Mexico over the last forty years, it now regularly nests in Bolsa Chica Ecological Reserve, a salt marsh in Orange County. Some skimmers come as far north as Venice Beach in Los Angeles—whether blown off track, just visiting, or new colonizers, only time will tell. Like terns, Black Skimmers are ground nesters. They require undisturbed dunes, where they build their nests by scraping a shallow depression in the sand. Their habitat is in short supply in Southern California, so it's surprising that Black Skimmers have moved into this region.

Black Skimmers hunt in the evening and early morning, and when the Grunion are running (see page 154), you may glimpse skimmers patrolling the beaches for a meal in the dark. Black Skimmers prey on all species of small, surface-dwelling fish, so the presence of a healthy skimmer population indicates how plentiful these fish are near a beach. Skimmers are named for the way they skim over water as they hunt. It is the only North American bird with a bottom bill that is much longer than the one on top. This adaptation allows the bird to slice through the water with only its lower bill in order to catch fish on the fly. Its bill is outlandishly big for its body, and seen head-on, the bill is laterally compressed—like a small sword or knife.

Although Black Skimmers and terns both have long tails and very small legs for their size, Black Skimmers are unmistakable. An adult looks as if it wears a spiffy black tuxedo over a white shirt: black wings and tail with a white throat and belly. Its head and neck are black, and it has a broad white bar across its face above its bill. A juvenile's wings and head are mottled brown and white, and they gradually darken over the first year. The juvenile's bill is duskier than the bright red and black bill of the adult. The size and color of the Black Skimmer's bill, its face with a white bar, and its black beady eyes give this spectacular bird a clownlike appearance.

Photographs and most descriptions do not convey how small a Black Skimmer is. Its body, including its long tail, is only about 14 inches long, but its bill adds another 6 to 7 inches to its length.

Black Skimmer (Rynchops niger) —Gary Kramer photo, U.S. Fish and Wildlife Service

A juvenile Black Skimmer at Venice Beach

PELICANS

California Brown Pelican (*Pelecanus occidentalis*)
White Pelican (*Pelecanus erythrorhynchos*)

The enormous bill, huge wingspan (6 to 7 feet), and fingerlike wing tips of the California Brown Pelican (*Pelecanus occidentalis*) make it easy to identify. Standing nearly 3 feet high, this bird is both magnificent and comical with its oversized bill and the pouch that hangs beneath it. Juveniles are uniformly silvery brown, but mature adults are lighter brown and have tan necks, pale yellow crowns, and tan pouches. When in full breeding plumage, the California Brown Pelican is spectacular. It has a dark brown neck, a golden crown, and a salmon-colored pouch that shades to dark green toward the tip.

The California Brown Pelican was a rare sight in the 1960s and '70s, but now these glorious fliers occur all along the Southern California coast. Their abundance is an environmental success story. California Brown Pelicans, and other common birds such as the California Condor (*Gymnogyps californianus*), sank to the edge of extinction when the insecticide DDT infiltrated the food chain. DDT caused their eggs to have such thin shells that they cracked when nesting mothers sat on them, causing the death of countless young birds. There were years when only a few eggs survived, but DDT was banned more than thirty years ago, and pelican populations have improved dramatically.

The White Pelican (*Pelecanus erythrorhynchos*) is 5 feet long, about a foot longer than the California Brown Pelican. Juveniles and adults have golden bills and legs and black secondary feathers. The secondaries are folded under the wing when the bird is resting and are only visible when the pelican is flying; therefore a resting White Pelican looks all white.

California Brown Pelicans (Pelecanus occidentalis); *juvenile on right and adult on left*

White Pelican
(Pelecanus
erythrorhynchos)
—John Foster photo,
U.S. Fish and Wildlife Service

California Brown Pelicans are not especially wary of humans. They may hunt waters close to surfers, beg or steal food from fishermen along wharves, and rest on rocks and sandbars near beachcombers. They congregate where they can sun and groom themselves, sometimes in huge numbers—one hundred or more. Most of the time, when floating or on land, a California Brown Pelican tucks its bill flat along its neck, but when in close quarters with other pelicans, it will lift its bill straight up to the sky, displaying its throat and neck to its neighbors. Given the length and narrowness of this pelican's bill, this is an odd sight.

California Brown Pelicans hunt together, and it is almost magical to see a squadron of a dozen or so birds disappear between ocean swells and reappear a moment later as they skim the waves. A pelican dives spectacularly as it fishes. It will make one or two loops above its quarry, then with wings folded back along its body it dives, hitting the water with breathtaking force. The pelican immediately bobs back to the surface like a huge cork. Its narrow bill helps the pelican slice through the water. Often gulls accompany pelicans when they dive and will try to steal the pelican's catch.

The White Pelican is more wary of humans and is far less common on the coast. It prefers a calm habitat and is occasionally seen where salt marshes give way to brackish or freshwater wetlands. White Pelicans fish cooperatively, forming a circle while they swim that traps schools of fish, which the pelicans then scoop from the water using their pouches as nets. Sometimes an individual California Brown Pelican will feed in this manner. Whether pelicans dive for fish or scoop them from the water, the fish often get stuck sideways in the pelican's pouch. The pelican must toss the fish until it can smoothly slide down its narrow throat.

Nonbreeding adult California Brown Pelican (Pelecanus occidentalis) in flight

A juvenile California Brown Pelican diving after fish

A breeding adult California Brown Pelican that just caught a fish in its pouch

CORMORANT

Double-Crested Cormorant (*Phalacrocorax auritus*)

In Southern California, Double-Crested Cormorants (*Phalacrocorax auritus*) are the most widespread and highly abundant species of the cormorant family. They are such expert fishers that anglers often resent them for "stealing" fish in stocked lakes and streams. Studies of pollution and overfishing indicate that the human impact on fish stock is greater than the cormorant impact. Nonetheless, in some parts of the United States government officials and private individuals use lethal control to destroy thousands of cormorants a year. This is ironic because these birds were placed on the endangered species list about thirty-five years ago, and in many regions their numbers still haven't recovered from centuries of persecution. Responsible anglers and environmentalists are working together to find solutions that meet the needs of anglers and cormorants, such as delaying the release of hatchery fish so they are too large for cormorants to prey on. The fact that people are developing nonlethal solutions to remedy cormorant overpopulation is a hopeful sign for the cormorant's future, because when one species dominates a habitat the way humans tend to, all species lose.

The cormorant is a diving bird, but like a duck it dives from a floating position. One moment it is drifting on the water, the next it has disappeared with only a small stream of bubbles indicating the direction it is traveling. It can swim for some distance underwater before surfacing for air, propelled by its powerful feet and aided by its streamlined body. It snags a tiny fish and brings it to the surface to swallow, tossing it into the air to get it in the right position so the fish simply slithers down the bird's throat.

Cormorants are large birds—about 3 feet long—that look a bit like loons when floating on the water, but a cormorant has a thinner neck, hooked bill, and smallish head. Juveniles are dark brown with a tan neck and breast, and adults are iridescent black. The Double-Crested Cormorant has bright yellow flesh rimming its bill. It gets its fanciful common name from the small pale feathers that curl up above its eyes during breeding season, forming tiny double "crests."

You might observe cormorants swimming in the surf or flying in loose flocks like oceangoing geese. Interestingly, unlike most other water birds, a cormorant's wings are not waterproof. You may see these birds perched on rocks or pilings with their wings spread—drying out.

Juvenile Double-Crested Cormorant (Phalacrocorax auritus)
with a freshly caught fish

Adult nonbreeding Double-Crested
Cormorant spreading its wings to dry

Birds of Rocky Shores

OYSTERCATCHERS

Black Oystercatcher (*Haematopus bachmani*)

Rocky shores appeal to gulls vying for dominance, cormorants drying their wings, and pelicans sunning themselves, but they also attract birds that are hunting for gastropods, mussels, snail eggs, sponges, tunicates, and the oceanic debris that collects in cracks and crevices along the shore. The feathers of the Black Oystercatcher (*Haematopus bachmani*) camouflage it well among surf-drenched rocks, but this bird is unmistakable: it looks like a crow at a masquerade with long pink stockings on its legs and a bright red bill. It is about the same size as a crow, too, about 1½ feet long. From a distance, juvenile and adult Black Oystercatchers look virtually identical, but a juvenile has subtle charcoal gray and brown mottling on its back and wings. The oystercatcher stumps along rocks foraging for invertebrates hidden in cracks and crevices and within mussel beds. It moves lightning fast when it has found prey and slices the prey's shell open with its knifelike bill. Listen for the Black Oystercatcher's lovely low whistles as it calls to its companions.

SANDPIPERS

Black Turnstone (*Arenaria melanocephala*)
Wandering Tattler (*Heteroscelus incanus*)

Turnstones are busy little birds, about 9 inches long, that scrounge around rocks and kelp wracks for small marine invertebrates. A turnstone has a slight indentation on top of its bill that helps it lift or flip small stones over to find prey. They are not particularly shy and will forage within a few yards of a person sitting quietly.

A Black Turnstone (*Arenaria melanocephala*) develops white stripes across its face above the bill during breeding season; the rest of the year it has a solid black head. Generally, the Black Turnstone is more common along the Southern California coast than the Ruddy Turnstone (*Arenaria interpres*), which has chestnut-colored wings and orangish yellow legs. When their wings are spread in flight, turnstones display a white stripe on the back and bold black-and-white-striped wings, which makes a flock of these birds one of the most dramatic sights on the beach.

The Wandering Tattler (*Heteroscelus incanus*) spends winter and spring in Southern California, flying all the way from Alaska. It seems quite content to forage for invertebrates along rocks near humans, occasionally shooting a curious glance our way. In breeding plumage, it has a speckled, gray and white breast and throat and yellow legs; in nonbreeding plumage, its throat and breast are gray and not mottled.

Black Oystercatcher (Haematopus bachmani)

Black Turnstone (Arenaria melanocephala)

Wandering Tattler (Heteroscelus incanus)

Birds of Sandy Beaches

SANDPIPERS

Willet (*Catoptrophorus semipalmatus*)

All along the water's edge there are small dimples, holes, and tiny mounds in the wet sand. As sandpipers scurry along sandy beaches, they look for these tracks because they are evidence of bean clams, sand crabs, sandworms, and marine invertebrates below the sand that make tasty meals. The presence of shorebirds indicates a healthy beach with a lot of wildlife diversity in the food web. Some sandpipers, such as Willets, periodically regurgitate the indigestible parts of the creatures they have eaten, leaving a wad of tiny shell fragments on the sand. The pellet can yield specific information about a sandpiper's diet, such as the species of mollusks or crustaceans it has recently eaten. It's really interesting to look at pellets since they can give you a good "snapshot" of local marine species that are otherwise hidden.

The Willet (*Catoptrophorus semipalmatus*), about 15 inches long, is the most common large sandpiper in Southern California. In winter, it has pale gray feathers and a charcoal gray bill that is a little longer than its head. In spring it develops black spots on its back. It looks very similar to the smaller Wandering Tattler (*Heteroscelus incanus*), but the Willet has gray legs.

Willets can be found on sandy beaches, rocky shores, and in coastal wetlands. Like all sandpipers, they follow the tides and feed when low tides leave long stretches of intertidal sand or mud exposed. At high tide, Willets take to high ground, such as undisturbed dunes and rocks, where they bide their time until the tide turns. The best time to view Willets is during early morning and late afternoon low tides, because there are fewer people and dozens of the birds gather to feed, sun, and groom themselves on the beach. This is also the time to see them foraging in small clusters of three or four individuals, whereas during the middle of the day they generally forage alone.

Willets are wary and will often take to the air even if you are 50 feet away, scattering and warning other birds of your approach with loud whistling cries. When in flight, this drab-looking bird displays bold black-and-white stripes on its wings.

Willet (Catoptrophorus semipalmatus) *in winter plumage*

Willets in the surf

Sandpipers search for invertebrates along the water's edge. This sand casting indicates the presence of a sandworm.

Sandpipers regurgitate the shells of invertebrates in small pellets.

Whimbrel (*Numenius phaeopus*)
Marbled Godwit (*Limosa fedoa*)
Surfbird (*Aphriza virgata*)

When the tide is out, sandpipers come to forage along the stretch of soft, squishy intertidal sand or mud that is exposed. They have long, thin bills they probe the sand with, looking for marine invertebrates like worms, sand crabs, and clams. The birds with longer bills can dig deeper, but at times they compete with the birds with shorter bills by picking closer to the surface. You can see them with their bills partly open, dipping into and flipping up wet sand. They use their bills like chopsticks to pick up the prey, then, with small, lightning-fast nibbling and tossing movements, they maneuver the prey to their mouths.

Both the Whimbrel (*Numenius phaeopus*) and Marbled Godwit (*Limosa fedoa*) visit Southern California in late summer, autumn, and winter. Both are about 18 inches long and buff colored with darker speckles, and they have striped heads with very long bills that are almost twice as long as their heads. However, the Whimbrel's bill is dark and curves down. The Whimbrel is something of a loner, and you can see it picking along rocks and digging into sand or soft mud.

The Marbled Godwit is more common in Southern California, and you are likely to see it on sandy beaches and coastal wetlands foraging with several other individuals. Its long reddish bill has a black tip and turns up at the end. Perhaps that's why the English named it "good" or "godly creature," because they thought its bill pointed "up to God." When in flight, the Marbled Godwit's rust-colored underwings are visible.

The Surfbird (*Aphriza virgata*), which could almost be called a "shore pigeon" because of its size and shape, is a winter visitor. Usually seen on or near rocks or breakwaters, this plump little bird has stumpy yellow legs, a short bicolored (gray and rust) bill, and a white breast with black freckles. Surfbirds are most often seen on or near rocks or breakwaters.

Whimbrel
(Numenius
phaeopus)

Marbled Godwits
(Limosa fedoa)

Surfbird
(Aphriza virgata)

Sanderling (*Calidris alba*)

Flocks of small sandpipers, commonly called *peeps,* wander and feed along shores, lagoons, and salt marshes. When they take flight, it is like witnessing an airborne school of fish. As they turn and maneuver, they change colors, alternately flashing their gray backs and white bellies, and their wings make a soft ruffling sound as they pass that makes the very air seem alive!

In North America there are over a dozen *Calidris* species, tiny members of the sandpiper family that are adapted to many different habitats from northern rocky shores in Alaska to inland prairies. None of them live in Southern California year-round; they migrate north for their breeding season. This means that most of the time (August through April) you can see a number of sandpipers in Southern California that are gray and white and lack any particularly obvious markings that set them apart.

The Sanderling (*Calidris alba*) is the most common sandpiper along the open coast. It is 8 inches long and better adapted to the rough weather of the seashore than other *Calidris* species. Even still, these cute birds seem terrified of the ocean as they scurry forward and back along the surf line just out of the reach of the waves, or instantaneously take to the air to avoid a wetting. Although sometimes they feed in loose groups of only a few birds, they more commonly forage in groups of ten to twenty or more individuals. Their little black legs twinkle along the sand as the waves chase them up the shore. Sometimes they run so quickly that their legs blur, and the birds look as though they are magically suspended above the sand.

Young Sanderlings have small, black diamond-shaped spots along their backs, which fade to a light gray as they mature. During breeding season their backs, wings, and heads turn reddish. Adults fly north to Canada in April to nest and raise young and return to Southern California toward the end of summer.

Sanderlings (Calidris alba)

Birds of Coastal Wetlands

SANDPIPERS

Least Sandpiper (*Calidris minutilla*)
Western Sandpiper (*Calidris mauri*)
Dunlin (*Calidris alpina*)
Dowitcher (*Limnodromus* species)

Coastal wetlands are invaluable places where many types of birds can hatch and raise young, rest while migrating, and find food. Most *Calidris* species, or *peeps,* are adapted to the calm water and milder weather of salt marshes, estuaries, lagoons, and other coastal wetlands and are not found on the open coast. The Least Sandpiper (*Calidris minutilla*) is the smallest; it is about 6 inches long—the size of a sparrow. Its species name, *minutilla,* is Latin for "tiny," and it is the only peep with yellow legs. At 6½ inches long, the Western Sandpiper (*Calidris mauri*) is only slightly bigger; it has black legs and a larger bill that curves down more than the Least Sandpiper's. Both these peeps look very much like their slightly larger relative the Sanderling (*Calidris alba*), especially in nonbreeding plumage when they all have grayish tan wings and white bellies. During breeding season adult Western and Least Sandpipers develop black spangles on their wings and their gray coloration turns tan and brown. Look for the yellow legs of the Least Sandpiper in order to tell them apart.

The Dunlin (*Calidris alpina*) is the size of a Sanderling, generally 8 inches long. A juvenile has a black belly and a chest and back that are streaked dark brown and tan. A nonbreeding adult is grayish tan with a white belly. During breeding season in early spring, the Dunlin develops a black belly and reddish splotches on its wings.

The dowitcher (*Limnodromus* species) is a plump sandpiper with bright yellowish green legs and a long, straight, stout bill. Other than a very slight difference in the length of their bills, the Long-Billed (*Limnodromus scolopaceus*) and Short-Billed Dowitcher (*Limnodromus griseus*) are virtually identical, and their flocks intermingle as they feed in Southern California coastal wetlands during winter. Nonbreeding birds of both species are speckled tan and brown above and gray below. Their throats and chests turn cinnamon red as breeding season approaches, but they move north and inland to nest so you won't see them in full breeding plumage along the coast. The dowitcher is a busy little bird that feeds in flocks, quickly jabbing its bill up and down into the mud as if it was playing tug-of-war with its prey—worms and other invertebrates. Look for dowitchers at lagoons and on shallow bays, such as the bay side of the Silver Strand State Beach in San Diego County, where thousands of shorebirds gather each year.

Left: *Least Sandpiper* (Calidris minutilla)

Right: *Western Sandpiper* (Calidris mauri) —Lee Karney photo, U.S. Fish and Wildlife Service

Dunlin (Calidris alpina) —Herbert Clarke photo

Dowitchers (Limnodromus *species*)

Inset: sandpiper tracks

PLOVERS

Black-Bellied Plover (*Pluvialis squatarola*)
Pacific Golden-Plover (*Pluvialis fulva*)
Killdeer (*Charadrius vociferus*)
Semipalmated Plover (*Charadrius semipalmatus*)

Many people call all the shorebirds they see on the beach "sandpipers." That's a fair assumption because most sandpipers live along the coast, and plovers live in coastal wetlands. However, plovers also visit beaches, and although species of the sandpiper and plover families are small, gray and white birds, they have distinguishing features and feeding behaviors. Plovers have larger eyes; shorter, stouter bills; and longer legs in proportion to their body size than sandpipers. Sandpipers stroll along the beach, but plovers run and then freeze as they look around for food; then they run again. Rather than probing into the sand the way sandpipers do, plovers tend to pick for insects and soft-bodied invertebrates along the surface of mud and muddy sand, or around rocks and wracks.

The Black-Bellied Plover (*Pluvialis squatarola*) seems a strange name for a bird that, when in Southern California at least, has a white belly! Because it heads north and inland to breed, Southern Californians rarely see it with its spectacular breeding plumage: black-and-white speckled back and solid black lower face and belly. The Pacific Golden-Plover (*Pluvialis fulva*) looks similar. Both species are about 1 foot long with a 2-foot wingspan. The Pacific Golden-Plover also has a short, stumpy tail, and in breeding regalia it has black- and gold-speckled wings. In nonbreeding plumage, the Pacific Golden-Plover has a faint wash of gold on its back and wings, and a belly that is grayer than the Black-Bellied Plover's. While in Southern California, both species have mottled grayish tan wings with a white rim around each feather, and pale bellies. Toward breeding season, the bottom half of their faces turn dark gray and the mottling on their wings darkens.

The Killdeer (*Charadrius vociferus*), 10 inches long; Semipalmated Plover (*Charadrius semipalmatus*), 7 inches long; and Snowy Plover (*Charadrius alexandrinus*), 6 inches long, all have brown coats, white bellies, and spiffy neck bands. The Killdeer has two brown neck bands, while the Semipalmated Plover has one, and the Snowy Plover has a single brown neck band that does not quite meet at the throat. The Semipalmated Plover is named for its semiwebbed feet.

Inset: *Pacific Golden-Plover* (Pluvialis fulva)
—Lee Karney photo, U.S. Fish and Wildlife Service

Top right: *Black-Bellied Plover* (Pluvialis squatarola)

Semipalmated Plover (Charadrius semipalmatus)
—Herbert Clarke photo

The Snowy Plover prefers flat dunes, where its light colors and diminutive size make it almost impossible to spot. It nests among Least Terns (*Sterna antillarum*). The Snowy Plover's numbers have plummeted because of urbanization, and it is listed as a federally threatened species. Southern California is struggling to hang onto a few breeding populations in its remaining coastal wetlands.

Killdeer (Charadrius vociferus)
—Photo courtesy of pdphoto.org

GREBES

Western Grebe (*Aechmophorus occidentalis*)
Clark's Grebe (*Aechmophorus clarkii*)
Horned Grebe (*Podiceps auritus*)
Eared Grebe (*Podiceps nigricollis*)

Although grebes are drab looking when they are in Southern California and are not in their breeding plumage, these little birds are very enjoyable to watch as they dive, bob on the water, and groom themselves, scratching their necks with their feet like a dog or fluffing out their feathers with a self-satisfied look. Grebes prefer quiet waters along bays, harbors, and coastal marshes. Not only are they fantastic divers, vanishing with barely a ripple, but occasionally you may see a grebe swimming with only its head above the water's surface like a tiny periscope, and like a periscope, the grebe will slowly and silently submerge its head.

When small fish are running, you may see squadrons of Western Grebes (*Aechmophorus occidentalis*) streaming in to hunt. As they float on the water they slowly surround a school. Suddenly, one by one, each bird dives and streaks underwater, pursuing the school as it splits and curves out of their reach. When an unwary fish breaks away from the safety of the school, a Western Grebe singles it out and snatches it up. To witness this exciting hunt, look for large numbers of anglers lining the fishing piers. They know when small fish are abundant, and Western Grebes will often be there as well. The Western Grebe is the largest grebe in Southern California, at about 2 feet long. Both it and the Clark's Grebe (*Aechmophorus clarkii*) look similar, but the Clark's Grebe has a brighter yellow bill and it has more white on its face.

Two smaller species of grebe spend winter in Southern California coastal wetlands, and occasionally they venture onto the open coast. The Horned Grebe (*Podiceps auritus*) and Eared Grebe (*Podiceps nigricollis*) are about 1 foot long, about half the size of the Western Grebe and Clark's Grebe. Horned and Eared Grebes are named for yellow feathers that extend along the sides of their heads during breeding season.

However, during summer these two grebes migrate to their northern nesting grounds—vanishing before their plumage becomes distinctive and colorful. While in Southern California both species look similar; they have dark gray upper parts and light gray and white faces, throats, and bellies. The Horned Grebe is more streamlined, has a flatter head, and a narrower bill, and floats lower in the water than the Eared Grebe. The Eared Grebe has a smaller, rounder head and body and less white on its face. Proportionately, these two species have slightly shorter necks than the Western Grebe and Clark's Grebe.

Inset:
Western Grebe
(Aechmophorus
occidentalis)

Clark's Grebe (Aechmophorus clarkii)
—Jim Krakowski photo, U.S. Fish and Wildlife Service

Nonbreeding Horned Grebe (Podiceps auritus)

Nonbreeding Eared Grebe (Podiceps nigricollis)

HERONS AND EGRETS

Great Blue Heron (*Ardea herodias*)
Great Egret (*Ardea alba*)

The Great Blue Heron (*Ardea herodias*) is fairly common near coastal wetlands, but to see one swoop down the beach is a breathtaking sight. Clothed in grayish blue feathers, it stands nearly 4 feet tall, has a 6-foot wingspan, and utters a spine-tingling, screamlike croak. It hunts slowly, freezing in place until flashing forward to capture its prey. Its neck strikes like a whip attached to the bird's still body. The Great Blue Heron is well adapted to many habitats: it hunts along seashores for fish and mollusks during low tides and when there are shallow waves, and it prowls fields near wetlands where it preys on small mammals, lizards, and amphibians. Other long-legged birds such as sandpipers, or large-bodied birds such as pelicans, nest on the ground, but the Great Blue Heron nests in trees—like a monster-sized scrub jay! When you see these huge birds struggling to maintain their balance, crashing their enormous wings against branches and sending showers of leaves and twigs to the ground, it's astonishing that they don't just give it up and settle on the ground to nest. Although solitary when fully grown, these birds tend to nest in groups called *heronries*. A heronry may include a dozen families, and it is quite a sight to observe these huge, beautiful birds screeching and calling as they carry prey to their babies.

The Great Egret (*Ardea alba*) was almost hunted to extinction in the nineteenth century for its long, white breeding plumage. Though its plumes may have made elegant hats for ladies, nothing can match the elegance and beauty of the living bird. It became a symbol for the Audubon Society, and the conservation of the Great Egret is one of the society's proudest achievements.

Found at fresh and saltwater marshes, the Great Egret slowly stalks through the water, freezes, bends over, and looks into the water for passing fish, which it stabs at with its bill. From a distance, people frequently confuse it with the Snowy Egret (*Egretta thula*). Both birds are pure white, long-legged waders, but the Great Egret is much larger—over 3 feet high. The Great Egret has black legs and feet, and its neck is longer than the Snowy Egret's, though this can be hard to see because both of these birds constantly retract and extend their flexible necks as they hunt and groom themselves. The bright yellow bill of the Great Egret is the most distinctive difference between the species when distance makes it hard to determine the size of the bird. You may see flocks of these birds sunning themselves on a warm morning, or stalking the water together and squabbling over a catch like gulls.

Great Blue Heron
(Ardea herodias)

Great Egret
(Ardea alba)

Great Egret
(foreground)
and Snowy Egret
(Egretta thula)

Snowy Egret (*Egretta thula*)

The Snowy Egret (*Egretta thula*) is much smaller, about 24 inches tall, and is more active than the Great Blue Heron or the Great Egret. It hurries along the banks of shallow waters, stirring up prey with its startling feet that look like yellow slippers; juveniles have yellow streaks up the back of their legs. Although beautiful, the Snowy Egret appears to have a comical side. Sometimes the breeding plumage on its head stands up like an unruly mop of hair. This bird can look like cotton candy on a stick when it hunches down and fluffs its feathers. It can also look graceful and svelte when it stretches out in search of prey.

The Snowy Egret isn't a picky eater and will swallow nearly anything it stirs up, including mollusks, other invertebrates, and fish that may be too small to draw the attention of larger wading birds. It is interesting to note how different birds swallow their meals. A sandpiper makes small nibbling movements with its bill to get the food from the tip of its beak to its mouth. Fish-eating ducks, cormorants, and pelicans toss their catch in the air to position prey so it slithers down their throats. Egrets and herons do this also, and it is surprising how many times they drop their prey and it escapes!

At salt marshes other herons often take advantage of the Snowy Egret's activity. A Great Egret may slowly walk behind a Snowy Egret and catch the fish that slide past it. On the other hand, there are times when the busy Snowy Egret seems to irritate a Great Egret by ruining its slow, deliberate hunting, inadvertently scaring off a tasty meal. The Great Egret may retaliate by screaming, squawking, and lunging at the Snowy Egret as if it was an annoying younger sibling. Most of the time these beautiful birds coexist peaceably, sometimes even sharing nesting and roosting sites in low trees.

Snowy Egret (Egretta thula)

DUCKS

Red-Breasted Merganser (*Mergus serrator*)
Surf Scoter (*Melannita perspicillata*)

In winter, when inland ponds and lakes are cold or frozen over, Southern California's coastal wetlands offer some freshwater ducks a warm, less harsh environment with good feeding grounds. Some regularly spend the winter on coastal lagoons and estuaries, and this is an excellent time for birding in Southern California. Common visitors include the scaup (*Aythya* species), Bufflehead (*Bucephala albeola*), American Widgeon (*Anas americana*), and Northern Shoveler (*Anas clypeata*), as well as the beautiful and ubiquitous Mallard (*Anas platyrhynchos*).

Most of these visiting ducks eat plant material and algae that grows year-round in Southern California's sunny climate. Without the ducks, this vegetation and algae would choke the wetlands. The Red-Breasted Merganser (*Mergus serrator*), however, has a specialized saw-edged bill that is perfect for seizing small fish. It lives year-round in Southern California's calm coastal wetlands. About 24 inches long, the size of a Mallard, the merganser's crown of spiked feathers and thin bill are distinctive. Nonbreeding males and females have reddish heads and gray wings and backs. The breeding male develops an iridescent dark green head, white neck, and chestnut breast (despite its common name its breast is not red). Its back becomes black and its wings develop small white patches. A merganser often paddles along with its head underwater, searching for fish.

During winter, Southern California commonly hosts the Surf Scoter (*Melannita perspicillata*), a duck that is adapted to life on the ocean and seems unperturbed by its gigantic swells. It dives from a floating position, feeding mostly on underwater bivalves. You may see it near a long fishing pier, or near rocky outcroppings where mollusks are abundant. The female is charcoal gray with lighter gray head patches, while the male is black except for a white patch on its forehead and on the back of its head. The adult male has a distinct bill: it is thick, has a hump on top like a Roman nose, and is orange and white except for two black circles that make this duck appear as if it has eyeglasses perched on its bill.

Male scaup
(Aythya *species*)

American Widgeons (Anas americana);
male in foreground.

Female Northern Shoveler (Anas clypeata)
—Dave Menke photo, U.S. Fish and Wildlife Service

A male (foreground) *and female Mallard*
(Anas platyrhynchos) *cleaning*

Red-Breasted Merganser (Mergus serrator)
—Dave Menke photo, U.S. Fish and Wildlife Service

Male Surf Scoter (Melannita perspicillata)
—Photo courtesy of Gulf of Farallones
National Marine Sanctuary Photo Library

RAPTORS

Turkey Vulture (*Cathartes aura*)
Red-Tailed Hawk (*Buteo jamaicensis*)
Osprey (*Pandion haliaetus*)

In the morning or on damp days, you may see raptors perched in trees or on telephone poles, hunched down and fluffing their feathers against the cold as they watch for prey near beaches or salt marshes. On warm afternoons, however, when updrafts make soaring easier, they leap into the air and wheel overhead looking for prey. Raptors are vital to a healthy environment. They keep small mammal populations in check and consume carrion.

Turkey Vultures (*Cathartes aura*) visit beaches when red tides or disease have killed marine creatures and currents have washed them to shore. Turkey Vultures do not usually kill other animals, though they may finish off one that is already dying. They are scavengers—nature's recyclers. By breaking down and consuming decaying bodies, they provide leftovers for smaller wildlife and help keep the environment clean. The Turkey Vulture is black with a gray tail and wings. Its head is small and shriveled, and adults have a red one while juveniles have a black head. Like all vultures, a Turkey Vulture's head is featherless— a necessary feature for its messy work. Turkey Vultures are over 2 feet long and have 5-foot wingspans.

Red-Tailed Hawks (*Buteo jamaicensis*) are adapted to all habitats across the United States. They perform the valuable function of keeping the small mammal population under control. However, they will also attack and eat other birds. This can make their presence problematic in salt marshes where there are endangered or threatened species. Juvenile Red-Tailed Hawks are brown and have a speckled brown and white belly. After about a year, adults develop reddish bellies and a red tail. A Red-Tailed Hawk has short yellow legs and a short, thick bill with a sharp downward curve. It stands about 18 inches high and has a 4-foot wingspan, but it appears larger because it is a chunky bird with very broad wings.

The Osprey (*Pandion haliaetus*), also known as the "fishing eagle," is specifically adapted to hunting fish in open water. Due to urban development it is rare to see one in Southern California, but an Osprey hunting over salt marshes and ocean shorelines is a magnificent sight. The Osprey is 2 feet long, has a white body with dark brown wings, a wingspan of about 5 feet, and a black-and-white checkerboard pattern on its tail. The Osprey's head is very distinctive: it's white, like a Bald Eagle's, but it has a thin band of black feathers along the sides.

Turkey Vulture
(Cathartes aura)
—Herbert Clarke photo

Immature Red-Tailed Hawk (Buteo jamaicensis)
—Lee Karney photo, U.S. Fish and Wildlife Service

Osprey (Pandion haliaetus) *at Chula Vista Nature Center* —Charles Gailband photo

RAIL

Light-Footed Clapper Rail (*Rallus longirostris levipes*)

The Light-Footed Clapper Rail (*Rallus longirostris levipes*) is a secretive bird that spends most of its time in the underbrush where its slim, "thin as a rail" body enables it to move with little telltale rustling. It only comes out into the open when the tide is out in the morning or early evening to search for California Horn Snails (*Cerithidea californica*) and Striped Shore Crabs (*Pachygrapsus crassipes*). This bird is about 14 inches long, has brown- and tan-streaked wings, gray and white bars on its flanks, and a reddish orange breast. It has a short tail that turns up; long legs; and a long, stout bill that curves down slightly. Light-Footed Clapper Rails are residents year-round. They nest and raise young in Cordgrass (*Spartina foliosa*) and Pickleweed (*Salicornia virginica*), where they find nesting material and shelter from predators such as hawks.

Unfortunately, a great deal of the plant life these birds depend on has been pushed out by the nonnative Ice Plant (*Carpobrotus edulis*), which arrived in Southern California hundreds of years ago in the ballast of a ship. Ice Plant is an attractive and adaptive plant that can grow almost anywhere. In the past it was deliberately planted to help stop dune erosion. However, it supports almost no native insects or invertebrates, much less birds or small mammals. Ecologically, Ice Plant habitats are virtually dead zones. Other introduced species, such as feral cats, red foxes, and dogs that are allowed off their leashes, have also taken a toll on the Light-Footed Clapper Rail, not to mention the impact these species have had on other native wildlife.

There are three subspecies of clapper rail in California and all three are endangered due to loss of habitat. The Light-Footed Clapper Rail is the only coastal salt marsh clapper rail in Southern California. It has been extirpated in Los Angeles County and there are only a few hundred pairs left in the rest of Southern California. The Newport Bay Ecological Reserve in Orange County, San Elijo Lagoon Ecological Reserve in northern San Diego County, and the Sweetwater Marsh National Wildlife Refuge in southern San Diego County near the Mexican border have nesting pairs.

Light-Footed Clapper Rail (Rallus longirostris levipes) —Herbert Clarke photo

SPARROW

Belding's Savannah Sparrow (*Passerculus sandwichensis beldingi*)

Small birds twitter in the undergrowth around coastal wetlands, darting in and out of view too quickly to identify at times. They could be towhees, jays, warblers, finches, phoebes, or hummingbirds—common upland birds that also make their homes near the coast. The Belding's Savannah Sparrow (*Passerculus sandwichensis beldingi*), however, is one small wetland bird that is specifically adapted to live in the Pickleweed (*Salicornia virginica*) of Southern California salt marshes. More heavily streaked than other savannah sparrows, the Belding's Savannah Sparrow has very dark black and white stripes on its chest, and tiny yellow feathers above its bill in front of its eyes. It is named for Lyman Belding, a nearly forgotten, self-taught, nineteenth-century ornithologist and collector of California birds.

The Belding's Savannah Sparrow is listed as an endangered species in California, and populations are severely stressed because of habitat loss, more than 90 percent of which has been urbanized in the last one hundred years. Although some birds, such as gulls, are quite adaptable, others have specific ecological niches and suffer because they are unable to adapt fast enough to the rapid changes caused by human development. The result is that these species have been forced into smaller and smaller geographical areas. For example, through biological changes over long ages of time, the Belding's Savannah Sparrow can only live in a salt marsh habitat, in Pickleweed that is cleaned, but not flooded, by periodic tidal flushing. Healthy saline wetlands normally have native Pickleweed in abundance. But if the habitat becomes too small or polluted, the Pickleweed disappears, and so does the Belding's Savannah Sparrow. Like so many other species, this savannah sparrow teeters on the edge of extinction. To some, its extinction may seem like a minor issue, just one less species of little streaky bird, but our joy in discovery would be diminished by that small amount. And its loss—or the loss of any species—impoverishes us all.

Belding's Savannah Sparrow (Passerculus sandwichensis beldingi) —Herbert Clarke photo

Resources

Marine Centers

From humble trailers to world class aquariums, each of the following marine centers is well worth a visit to learn more about Southern California coastal wildlife, and to get up close and personal with marine creatures through touch tanks and displays. Additional displays and information can be found at each county's natural history museum.

LOS ANGELES COUNTY

Aquarium of the Pacific
100 Aquarium Way, Long Beach, 90802
Phone: 562-590-3100
www.aquariumofpacific.org

Cabrillo Marine Aquarium
3720 Stephen White Drive, San Pedro, 90731
Phone: 310-548-7562
www.cabrilloaq.org

Heal the Bay's Santa Monica Pier Aquarium
1600 Ocean Front Walk, Santa Monica, 90401
Phone: 310-393-6149
www.healthebay.org

Roundhouse Marine Studies Lab and Aquarium
Manhattan Beach Pier, Manhattan Beach, 90266
Phone: 310-379-8117
www.roundhousemb.com

ORANGE COUNTY

Bolsa Chica Ecological Reserve Interpretive Center
3842 Warner Ave., Huntington Beach, 92469-4263
Phone: 714-846-1114
www.bolsachica.org

**Doheney State Beach Aquariums
and Interpretive Center**
25300 Dana Point Harbor Drive, Dana Point, 92629
Phone: 949-496-6172
www.dohenystatebeach.org

Muth Interpretive Center
2301 University Drive, Newport Beach, 92660
Phone: 949-923-2290
www.newportbay.org/muthover.htm

SAN DIEGO COUNTY

Birch Aquarium at Scripps
2300 Expedition Way, La Jolla, 92037
Phone: 858-534-FISH
www.aquarium.ucsd.edu

Cabrillo National Monument
1800 Cabrillo Memorial Drive, San Diego, 92106
Phone: 619-222-8211
www.nps.gov/cabr

Chula Vista Nature Center
1000 Gunpowder Point Drive, Chula Vista, 91910
Phone: 619-409-5900
www.chulavistanaturecenter.org

SeaWorld
500 SeaWorld Drive, San Diego, 92109
Phone: 800-380-3203
www.seaworld.com/seaworld/ca

Torrey Pines State Reserve
Between La Jolla and Del Mar on Highway 101, San Diego
Phone: 858-755-2063
www.torreypine.org

SANTA BARBARA COUNTY

Sea Center
211 Stearns Wharf, Santa Barbara, 93101
Phone: 805-682-4711
www.sbnature.org

Channel Islands National Park
1901 Spinnaker Drive, Ventura, 93001-4354
Phone: 805-658-5730
www.nps.gov/chis

Organizations

The following organizations offer information and education, and membership and volunteer opportunities.

American Cetacean Society
(Whale and dolphin conservation and education)
Phone: 310-548-6279
www.acsonline.org

Audubon—California
(Birding and conservation)
Phone: 626-564-1300
www.ca.audubon.org

California Coastal Commission
(Coastal Cleanup Day, third Saturday in September)
www.coastal.ca.gov

Heal the Bay
(Protection and cleanup of coastal waters,
   and watershed education)
Phone: 800-HEALBAY (in California only) or 310-453-0395
www.healthebay.org

Marine Mammal Care Center
(Rescue center)
Phone: 310-548-5677
www.mar3ine.org

Nature Conservancy—California Chapter
(Conservation)
www.tnccalifornia.org

Surfrider Foundation
(Protection of ocean, waves, and beaches)
Phone: 800-743-SURF
www.surfrider.org

U.S. Fish and Wildlife—Pacific Region
www.r1.fws.gov

Selected Bibliography

★ recommended reading and/or Web site

Books

Abbott, R. Tucker. 1954. *American Seashells*. New York: Van Nostrand Company.

———. 1985. *Seashells of the World*. New York: Golden Press, Western Publishing Company.

★ ———. 1986. *Seashells of North America*. New York: Golden Press, Western Publishing Company.

Barnhart, Diana, Vicki Leon, and Frank Balthis. 1995. *Tidepools: The Bright World of the Rocky Shoreline*. Inglewood, NJ: Silver Burdett Press.

★ Brown, Vinson. 1980. *The Amateur Naturalist's Handbook*. New York: Prentice Hall Press.

Brown, Vinson, and Henry G. Weston Jr. 1986. *Handbook of California Birds,* 3rd edition. Happy Camp, CA: Naturegraph Publishers, Inc.

★ California Coastal Commission. 2001. *California Access Guide,* revised edition. Berkeley: University of California Press.

Crump, Donald J., ed. 1985. *America's Seashore Wonderlands*. Washington, DC: National Geographic Society.

Dana, Richard Henry. 1964. *Two Years Before the Mast*. New York: The Modern Library.

Darling, Jim. 1999. *Gray Whales*. Stillwater, MN: Voyageur Press.

Ditmars, Elsa, and Anne Tatgenhorst. 2001. *California Coastal Adventures: A Guide to Beaches, Boat Trips, Islands, and Maritime Museums (Trailing Louis L'Amour)*. Palos Verdes, CA: Pacific Heritage Books.

Durrell, Gerald Malcolm. 1989. *The Practical Guide for the Amateur Naturalist*. New York: Alfred A. Knopf.

Durrenberger, Robert, Lorraine Peterson, and Keith Wilson. 1963. *California and the Western States*. Northridge, CA: Roberts Publishing Company.

Farrand, John Jr., ed. *The Audubon Society Master Guide to Birding,* vols. 1–3. 1985. New York: Alfred A. Knopf.

Fritzsche, R. A., R. H. Chamberlain, and R. A. Fisher. 1985. *Species profiles: Life histories and environmental requirements of coastal fishes and invertebrates (Pacific Southwest)*. U.S. Fish and Wildlife Service Biological Report 82(11/28). U.S. Army Corps of Engineers, TR EL-82-4.

★ Gray, Mary Taylor. 1999. *Watchable Birds of California*. Missoula, MT: Mountain Press Publishing.

Heimlich, Sara, and James Boran. 1994. *Killer Whales*. Stillwater, MN: Voyageur Press.

Hogue, Charles L. 1993. *Insects of the Los Angeles Basin.* Los Angeles, CA: Natural History Museum of Los Angeles County.

★ Holloway, Joel Ellis. 2003. *Dictionary of Birds of the United States.* Portland, OR: Timber Press.

Lorenzen, Bob. 2002. *Hiking the California Coastal Trail,* vol. 2: Monterey to Mexico. Mendocino, CA: Bored Feet Press.

McKenzie, Michelle, ed. 2002. *The Insider's Guide to the Monterey Bay Aquarium.* Monterey, CA: Monterey Bay Aquarium Foundation.

Melville, Herman. *Moby Dick; A Norton Critical Edition.* Hershel Parker and Harrison Hayford, eds. 1967. New York: W. W. Norton and Company.

O'Dell, Scott. 1960. *Island of the Blue Dolphins.* Boston: Houghton Mifflin Company.

Payne, Roger. 1995. *Among Whales.* New York: Charles Scribner's Sons.

Peterson, Roger Tory. "Audubon Birds of North America, Fifty Selections with Commentaries." New York: Macmillan Company. (A set of Audubon prints with Peterson's commentary on back of each one.)

Pryor, Karen, and Kenneth S. Norris, eds. 1998. *Dolphin Societies: Discoveries and Puzzles.* Berkeley: University of California Press.

★ Ricketts, Edward, Jack Calvin, and Joel W. Hedgpeth. 1992. *Between Pacific Tides,* 5th edition. Stanford, CA: Stanford University Press.

Santa Barbara Visitors Guide. 2003–4. Los Angeles: Striker Media Group.

★ Schad, Jerry. 2000. *Afoot and Afield in Los Angeles County,* 2nd edition. Berkeley, CA: Wilderness Press.

Sept, J. Duane. 2002. *The Beachcomber's Guide to Seashore Life of California.* Madeira Park, British Columbia, Canada: Harbour Publishing.

Sibley, David Allen. 2000. *The Sibley Guide to Birds.* NY: Alfred A. Knopf.

★ ———. 2003. *The Sibley Field Guide to Birds of Western North America.* New York: Alfred A. Knopf.

★ Udvardy, Miklos D.F. *The Audubon Society Field Guide to North American Birds (Western Region).* 1986. New York: Alfred A. Knopf.

Web Sites

BIRDS

American Ornithologists' Union. Check-List of North American Birds, 7th edition. http:www.aou.org

GENERAL INFORMATION

Birch Aquarium at Scripps, San Diego. http://www.aquarium.ucsd.edu

British Marine Life Study Society.
http://ourworld.compuserve.com/homepages/BMLSS/Homepage.html

★ Cabrillo Marine Aquarium. http://www.cabrilloaq.org

California State University, Fullerton; Department of Biological Science.
http://biology.fullerton.edu/

Enchanted Learning. http://www.enchantedlearning.com

The Field Museum. http://www.fieldmuseum.org/

National Oceanic and Atmospheric Administration, National Marine Sanctuary Program; Long Term Monitoring Program and Experiential Training for Students (LiMPETS). http://limpets.noaa.gov/naturalhistory/welcome.html (information on the natural history and habitat of Channel Island species)

Natural History Museum of Los Angeles County. www.nhm.org

★ U.S. Fish and Wildlife Service. http:www.fws.gov (fisheries and habitat conservation, images, birds, and endangered species)

★ U.S. Geological Survey. Alphabetical Index of USGS Science Categories. http://answers.usgs.gov/AtoZIndex.htm (information and maps on coastal ecosystems and individual species)

U.S. Geological Survey. USGS Water Resources of California. http://ca.water.usgs.gov (information on California water systems and projects)

★ University of California, Berkeley. Digital Library Project. http://elib.cs.berkeley.edu

★ University of California, Berkeley; Museum of Paleontology. UCMP Taxon Lift. www.ucmp.berkeley.edu/help/taxaform.html (information on plant and animal species)

★ University of California, Santa Barbara. The Love Lab. www.id.ucsb.edu/lovelab/

University of California, Santa Cruz. Institute of Marine Science. http://ims.ucsc.edu/

INVERTEBRATES

Australian Museum Online. The Invertebrates Collection. www.amonline.net.au/invertebrates/collection/index.htm

Bourquin, Avril. Man and Mollusk. http://manandmollusc.net/ (mollusk-related teacher and student resources, photos, and information)

California Information Node. Invasive Species. http://cain.nbii.gov

The Crustacean Society. http:www.vims.edu/tcs/

Gershwin, Lisa-Ann. 2002. Medusozoa. http:www.medusozoa.com/hydrozoa.html (information on jellies)

Hardy, Eddie. Hardy's Internet Guide to Marine Gastropods. www.gastropods.com

Humboldt State University. "North Coast Intertidal Guide: Chitons and Relatives." http://www.humboldt.edu/~intertid/cht/chiton.html

KeepersWeb.org. Shorekeepers' Animals. http://www.keepersweb.org/Shorekeepers/Animals/index.htm (information about and images of Pacific Coast species)

Moran, Amy L. 1997. Spawning and larval development of the black turban snail *Tegula funebralis* (Prosobranchia: Trochidae. *Marine Biology* 128(1): 107–14. http://www.marine.unc.edu/ALM.html

Moran, Amy L., and R. B. Emlet. 2001. Offspring size and performance in variable environments: Field studies on a marine snail. *Ecology* 82(6): 1597–1612. http://www.marine.unc.edu/ALM.html

Moran, Amy L., and D. T. Manahan. 2003. Energy metabolism during larval development of two abalone species, *Haliotis fulgens* and *H. sorenseni*. *Biological Bulletin* 204:270-277. http://www.marine.unc.edu/ALM.html

Moran, Amy L., and D. T. Manahan. 2004. Physiological recovery from prolonged starvation in larvae of the Pacific oyster *Crassostrea gigas*. *Journal of Experimental Marine Biology and Ecology* 306:17-36. http://www.marine.unc.edu/ALM.html

Negus, Rick. Sea Shells of California and Baja Mexico. http:www.californiashells.com

The Ohio State University, Division of Molluscs; Museum of Biological Diversity, Department of Evolution, Ecology, and Organismal Biology. http://www.biosci.ohio-state.edu/~molluscs/murex28/index.htm (information about and photographs of *Murex* species)

Omne vivum. http://www.omne-vivum.com (database that includes mollusk information)

★ Rudman, Bill; Australian Museum. Sea Slug Forum. http:www.seaslugforum.net

Schuchert, Peter. January 2005. Hydrozoa Directory. http://www.ville-ge.ch/musinfo/mhng/hydrozoa/hydrozoa-directory.htm

★ Selected Chitons of the West Coast of United States and Canada. http://home.inreach.com/burghart/wcoast.html (excerpts from *A Collector's Guide to West Coast Chitons*. 1969. Burghardt, Glenn and Laura. San Francisco Aquarium Society Publications.)

Stachowicz Lab; University of California, Davis. Bryozoans of the West Coast of North America. http://convoluta.ucdavis.edu/gallery/view_album.php?set_albumName=West_Coast_Bryozoans (photo gallery)

Stachowicz Lab Web site; University of California, Davis. "Ascidians of the West Coast of North America." http://www.ascidians.com/localities/namerica.htm (information about tunicates)

Tellinidae. http://www.chez.com/malacos/htm/R35.HTM (information about tellins)

University of California, San Diego. "Venomous Marine Animals of Southern California." http://www.health.ucsd.edu/poison/marine.asp

★ Washington State University Tri-Cities Natural History Museum, Gladys Archerd Shell Collection. http://nighthawk.tricity.wsu.edu/museum/ArcherdShellCollection/ShellCollection.html

Werry, Kerry L. British Columbia Creature Page. http://www3.bc.sympatico.ca/kerryw/creature/creat.htm (conchology and intertidal creatures)

★ Wrobel, Dave. The Jellies Zone. http://jellieszone.com

MAMMALS AND FISH

Alaska Fisheries Science Center, National Marine Fisheries Service and National Marine Mammals Lab. http:www.afsc.noaa.gov

American Cetacean Society. http:www.acsonline.org

America Zoo. http://www.americazoo.com/goto/index/mammals/classification.htm

California Department of Fish and Game. http:www.dfg.ca.gov

Fishbase. http:www.fishbase.org (relational database with information about all fish known to science)

Fishing Network, Southern California Edition. http:www.fishingnetwork.net

National Oceanic and Atmospheric Administration, National Marine Fisheries Service. www.nmfs.noaa.gov

Occidental College, Los Angeles; TOPS Program. http://departments.oxy.edu/tops/marinebio (photographs and information about Southern California marine animals)

Pacific Fishery Management Council. http:www.pcouncil.org

Pepperdine University; Grunion.org. http:www.grunion.org

Shaw, W. N., and T. J. Hassler. 1989. *Species Profiles: Life Histories and Environmental Requirements of Coastal Fishes and Invertebrates* (Pacific southwest): Pismo clam. U.S. Fish and Wildlife Service. http://www.nwrc.usgs.gov/publications/specintro.htm (information about many fish and invertebrate species.)

TAXONOMY

Brands, Sheila; Universal Taxonomic Services. The Taxonomicon, Systema Naturae 2000. http://www.taxonomicon.net/ (index of the world's past and present biota)

Cummins, R. Hays; School of Interdisciplinary Studies, Miami University. "The 'Nuts and Bolts' of Taxonomy and Scientific Classification." http://jrscience.wcp.muohio.edu/lab/TaxonomyLab.html

ITIS (Integrated Taxonomic Information System). http://www.itis.usda.gov (taxonomic information about North American species)

Index

abalone, 84
  Pink Abalone, 82–83
  Red Abalone, 82–83
Acanthina species, 102–3
Acanthodoris rhodoceras, 110–11
Acmaea
  insessa, 88
  mitra, 88–89
adductor muscles (bivalves), 12–13, 28
Aechmophorus
  clarkii, 220–21
  occidentalis, 220–21
Agloaphenia species, 58–59
Alaska, 184, 208, 214
algae, 130, 142
  animals it grows on, 88, 100
  animals that feed on, 26, 46, 80, 82,
    84, 94, 132, 160, 226
  brown, 60–61
  Encrusting Coralline Algae, 88, 98
  and red tides, 8, 144
  symbiotic, 116
algal bloom, 144
Amiantis callosa, 28–29
Amphistichus argenteus, 156–57, 162
Anas
  americana, 226–27
  clypeata, 226–27
  platyrhynchos, 226–27
anemone nurseries, 114
anemones, 11, 46, 118 148, 150
  Aggregating Anemone, 114–15
  compared to urchins, 132
  predators of, 92, 110
  shelter for, 72, 78
  Sunburst Anemone, 116–17
annelids, 118–19
Anomia peruviana, 16, 40–41
Año Nuevo State Reserve, 174
Anthopleura
  elegantissima, 114–15
  sola, 116–17

aperture (gastropods), 13
Aphriza virgata, 212–13
Aplysia californica, 108–9
Ardea
  alba, 222–25
  herodias, 222–25
Arenaria
  interpres, 208
  melanocephala, 208–9
Argopecten ventricosus, 42–43
Aristotle's lantern, 52, 132
arthropods
  definition of, 11
  of nearshore waters, 152–53
  of rocky shores, 120–29
  of sandy beaches, 54–57, 68–69
Asterina miniata, 130–31
Atlantic Ocean, 24, 38, 152
Audubon Society, 222
Aurelia labiata, 150–51
axis (gastropods), 13
Aythya species, 226–27

Baby's Ear, Western, 50–51
bacteria, 26, 42, 80, 144,
Baja California, Mexico, 50, 184
Balaenoptera musculus, 184
Balanus species, 120–21
baleen, 186
bands (bivalves), 12–13
barnacles, 2, 3, 11, 118
  acorn, 120–21
  attaching surfaces for, 84, 86, 100, 184
  Buckshot Barnacle, 120–21
  Goose-Neck Barnacle, 122–23
  Pelagic Barnacle, 122–23
  predators of, 102
  shelter for, 72
  Volcano Barnacle, 120–21
  where to find, 10
beachcombing, 7, 16, 86

beaches. *See individual beach names*
Belding, Lyman, 232
bell (jellies), 11
Bering Strait, 184, 187
birds, 11, 46, 60
    of coastal wetlands, 216–33
    nearshore, 190–207
    of rocky shores, 208–9
    of sandy beaches, 210–15
bivalves, 16, 166, 168, 190, 226
    characteristics of, 13
    definition of, 12
    free-swimming, 42–45
    rock-boring, 78
    rock-dwelling, 72–79
    sand-dwelling, 18–41
Blepharipoda occidentalis, 56–57
Bolsa Chica State Beach, x
Bolsa Chica Ecological Reserve, 189, 200
British Columbia, 174
bryozoans, 66, 68–69, 80, 96, 97, 102, 110
Bucephala albeola, 226–27
Bufflehead, 226–27
Bursa californica, 14, 100–101
Buteo jamaicensis, 228–29
butterfly shell, 22
byssal threads, 26, 40, 72
By-the-Wind Sailor, 148–49

Cabrillo Beach, 124
calcium carbonate, 38, 40
Calidris
    alba, 214–15, 216
    alpina, 216–17
    mauri, 216–17
    minutilla, 216–17
California Bight, x, 1, 60
California Department of Fish and Game,
    26, 30
California State Marine Fish
    (Garibaldi), 160
Calliostoma ligatum, 98–99
Canada, 214
Cancer species, 128–29
carapace, 56, 128, 129, 153
Carcharodon carcharias, 170
Carpinteria State Beach, x, 176
Carpobrotus edulis, 230
carrion, 92, 228
casting, sand, 211
Catalina Island, 185
Cathartes aura, 228–29

Catoptrophorus semipalmatus, 210–11
Cephaloscyllium ventriosum, 172–73
cerata (sea slugs), 110
Cerithidea californica, 46–47, 66, 230
cetaceans, 178
Chama arcana, 76–77
Channel Islands, x, 174, 184
Charadrius
    alexandrinus, 218
    semipalmatus, 218–19
    vociferus, 218–19
Chione
    californiensis, 30–31
    fluctifraga, 30–31
    species, 16
    undatella, 30–31, 32
Chiton, Mossy, 80–81
Chlamys rubida, 42–43
Chondrichthyes, 11
chordates, 146
    definition of, 11
    of nearshore waters, 154–87
    of rocky shores, 136–39
Chrysaora
    colorata, 150–51
    fuscescens, 150–51
Chthamalus dalli, 120–21
Chula Vista Nature Center, 229
Chumash tribe, 82, 170, 178
Cirolana harfordi, 124–25
clamming, 30
clams, 2, 5, 8, 16, 48, 58, 212
    bean, 10, 18–19, 20, 58, 59, 190, 210
    behavior of, 18
    California Jackknife, 24–25
    File Clam, 44
    hazards of eating, 30
    identification of, 28
    life cycle of, 26, 32
    lifespan of, 20
    Nuttall's Clam, 20–21
    Pacific Butter Clam, 28–29, 36
    Pismo Clam, 26–27
    Rosy Jackknife, 24–25
    of sandy beaches, 18–41
    siphons of, 18–19, 36, 172
    Sunset Clam, 20–21
Clapper Rail, Light-Footed, 230–31
Clinocardium nuttalii, 34–35
Clytia bakeri, 58–59
cnidarians
    definition of, 11
    of nearshore waters, 148–51

of rocky shores, 114–17
of sandy beaches, 58–59
Cockle
Nuttall's, 34–35
Pacific, 34–35
Rock, 32
collecting. *See* beachcombing
colonial nesters, 198
Condor, California, 202
Cone, California, 106–7
Conus californicus, 106–7
Convict Fish, 162
Coralline, Encrusting, 88, 98
Corambe, Frost-Spot, 68–69
Corambe pacifica, 68–69
Cordgrass, 230
cormorant family, 206
cormorants, 192, 208, 224
Double-Crested Cormorant, 206–7
Coronado, 2, 174
Coronado State Beach, 24
Cowrie, Chestnut, 92–93
crabs, 11, 72, 120
Mole Crab, 56
Pacific Sand Crab, 56–57
predators of, 112, 190
prey of, 94
Rock Crab, 128–29
sand, 10, 16, 56–57: handling of, 7;
predators of, 156, 166, 168, 190,
210, 212
Sheep Crab, 152–53
shelter for, 78
Shield-Back Kelp Crab, 66–67
Spiny Sand Crab, 56–57
Striped Shore Crab, 128–29, 230
true, 54, 128–29
See also hermit crabs
Crassostrea
gigas, 76–77
virginica, 76–77
Crepidula
adunca, 90–91
grandis, 90–91
onyx, 90–91
Crepipatella
dorsata, 90–91
lingulata, 90–91
crows, 198
crustaceans
characteristics of, 11, 124, 128, 152
habitat of, 60

planktonic, 142
predators of, 162, 166, 170, 174, 210
See also arthropods
Cryptolepas rhachianecti, 184
cucumber. *See* sea cucumbers
Cup-and-Saucer shells, 90
cuttlefish, 112
Cypraea spadicea, 92–93

Dana Point, x, 1
DDT, 202
Delphinus
capensis, 180
delphis, 180
species, 178, 183
Dendraster excentricus, 52–53
denticles, dermal, 170
Diadora aspera, 84–85
diatoms, 60, 142–43, 144
dinoflagellates, 60, 142–43, 144
Diogenidae, 5
Discurria insessa, 64 65
dissolved oxygen, 142, 144
Dogwinkle, 102, 104–5
dolphins, 11, 164, 186
Bottlenose Dolphin, 178–81
Common Dolphin, 178–80, 183
Long-Beaked Dolphin, 180
Pacific White-Sided Dolphin, 178, 182–83
Risso's Dolphin, 178, 182–83
Saddleback Dolphin, 180
Short-Beaked Dolphin, 180
dome (jellies), 11, 150
domoic acid, 144
Donax species, 18–19
dowitchers, 216–17
Long-Billed Dowitcher, 216
Short-Billed Dowitcher, 216
ducks, 206, 224, 226–27
Dunlin, 216–17

eagle, fishing (Osprey), 228–29
echinoderms, 146
definition of, 11–12
of rocky shores, 130–35
of sandy beaches, 52–53
echolocation, 180
Ectoprocta, 68
Eel, California Moray, 164–65
Eggcockle, Pacific, 34–35
Egregia species, 64–65

Egret
 Great, 222–23, 224
 Snowy, 222, 223, 224–25
Egretta thula, 222, 223, 224–25
El Niño, 60
Emerita analoga, 56–57
Emma Wood State Beach, x, 5
endangered species, 6, 198, 206, 228, 232
Enteroctopus dofleini, 112
epifaunal, 40
Eschrichtius robustus, 178, 184–87
Euphausia superba, 142–43
Euspira lewisii, 48–49
exoskeleton, 11, 152
extinction, 232

farming, commercial, 76, 82, 102
filter feeders, 30
finches, 232
fish, 188
 birds that prey on, 200, 205, 206,
  220, 222, 224, 226
 bony, 11, 136–39, 154–65
 camouflage for, 146
 cartilaginous, 11, 62, 166–73
 predators of, 52, 112
 prey of, 46, 144
 schools of, 156, 157, 204, 220
 shelter for, 78
fishing, 30, 154, 156, 162, 206
fish kill, 144
fission, 114
Fissurella volcano, 84–85
Flabellina iodinea, 110–11
flukes, 186–87
foot (gastropods), 13
fossils, 32–33
Frog Shell, California, 14, 100–101

Gaper, Pacific, 36–37
Garibaldi, 160–61
Gari californica, 20–21
gastropods, 12, 54, 78, 116, 208
 characteristics of, 13–14
 flat-shelled, 82–93
 growth of, 100
 of rocky shores, 68–69, 82–111
 of sandy beaches, 46–51, 66
 spiral-shelled, 82, 94–107
 without shells, 68–69, 108–11
Geukensia demissa, 38–39
Girella nigricans, 136–37

global warming, 144
Godwit, Marbled, 212–13
Golden-Plover, Pacific, 218–19
Grampus griseus, 178–79, 182–83
Grebe
 Clark's, 220–21
 Eared, 220–21
 Horned, 220–21
 Western, 220–21
ground nesters, 200
Grunion, 154–55
grunion run, 154–55
Guitarfish, 166–67
gull lines. *See* byssal threads
gulls, 62, 153, 189, 198, 208, 232
 Bonaparte's Gull, 194–95
 California Gull, 192–94
 Glaucous-Winged Gull, 192–93
 Heerman's Gull, 194–95
 Herring Gull, 192–93
 Ring-Billed Gull, 194–95
 Western Gull, 189, 191, 192–93
Gymnogyps californianus, 202
Gymnothorax mordax, 164–65

habitat loss, 2, 188–89, 198, 219, 232
Haematopus bachmani, 208–9
Half-Slipper, Pacific, 90–91
Haliotis
 corrugata, 82–83
 rufescens, 82–83
hawks, 230
 Red-Tailed Hawk, 228–29
Hermissenda crassicornis, 110–11
hermit crabs, 98, 106, 116
 Blueband Hermit Crab, 126–27
 Hairy Hermit Crab, 126–27
 Moon Snail Hermit Crab, 50, 54–55
Heron, Great Blue, 222–23, 224
Heterodontus francisci, 170–71
Heteroscelus incanus, 208–9
Hinnites giganteus, 44–45
home scar, 64–65, 80, 86
Horn Snail, California, 46–47, 66, 230
human impacts, 6
hummingbirds, 232
Huntington Beach, 2
hydroids, 11, 66, 72, 96, 110, 148
 Clam Hydroid, 58–59
 Plume Hydroid, 58–59
 Turgid Hydroid, 58–59
Hypsypops rubicundus, 160–61

Ice Plant, 230
Idotea wosnesenskii, 68–69
Indians, coastal, 38, 74, 82, 170, 178
intertidal zone, 8, 9, 10
introduced species, 24, 38, 76, 230
iridescence, 38
Isocheles pilosus, 48, 54–55
isopods, 11
    Kelp Isopod, 68–69
    Olive-Green Isopod, 68–69
    Scavenging Isopod, 124–25

Jackknife
    California, 24–25
    Rosy, 24–25
Jack Mackerel, Pacific, 156–57
jays, 232
jellies, 11, 146
    By-the-Wind Sailor, 148–49
    Moon Jelly, 150–51
    Purple-Striped Jelly, 150–51
    Sea Nettle, 150–51
jellyfish. *See* jellies
Jewel Box, Agate, 76–77
Jingle, Pearly, 16, 40–41

Kelletia kelleti, 100–101
kelp, 44, 58, 60–69, 118, 132, 158
    Feather Boa Kelp, 64–65
    Giant Kelp, 60–62
    wildlife on or around: arthropods,
        68–69, 122; birds, 196; bryozoans,
        68–69; cnidarians, 58; fish, 156,
        158, 160, 162, 172; mollusks, 64–67,
        68–69, 96
    wracks, 61, 64, 68, 172, 190, 208:
        definition of, 60; functions of, 62
Kelp Isopod, 68–69
Kelp Lace, 68–69
Kelp Limpet, 64–65, 88
keyhole limpets, 120
    Giant Keyhole Limpet, 84–85
    Rough Keyhole Limpet, 84–85
    Volcano Limpet, 84–85
    See also limpets
Killdeer, 218–19
knuckle-ridge (Gray Whale), 184
krill, 142–43, 146, 184

Laevicardium substriatum, 34–35
Lagenorhynchus obliquidens, 178–79, 182–83
La Jolla, x, 71, 176

Larus
    argentatus, 192–93
    californicus, 192–93, 194
    delawarensis, 194–95
    glaucescens, 192–93
    heermanni, 194–95
    occidentalis, 189, 191, 192–93
    philadelphia, 194–95
Latin America, 196
Leo Carrillo State Beach, 4
Lepas anatifera, 122–23
Leporimetis obesa, 22–23
Leptopecten latiauratus, 44–45, 66
Leuresthes tenuis, 154–55
Ligia occidentalis, 124–25
Lima, Hemphill's, 16, 44–45
Lima hemphilli, 16, 44–45
Limnodromus
    griseus, 216
    scolopaceus, 216
    species, 216–17
Limosa fedoa, 212–13
limpets, 72, 90, 120
    File Limpet, 88–89: albino, 88–89
    Finger Limpet, 88–89
    Giant Owl Limpet, 86–87
    Kelp Limpet, 64–65, 88
    Rough Limpet, 88–89
    White Cap Limpet, 88–89
    See also keyhole limpets
lions, sea. *See* sea lions
Lithothamnion species, 88, 98
Littleneck
    Pacific, 32–33, 34
    Rough-Sided, 12, 32–33
Littorina
    keenae, 94–95
    scutulata, 94–95
lobsters, 11, 54
    California Spiny Lobster, 152–53
Los Angeles, 188, 200
Lottia
    digitalis, 88–89
    gigantea, 86–87
    limatula, 88–89
    scabra, 88–89
Loxorhynchus grandis, 152–53
Lunatia lewisi, 48–49

Mackerel, Pacific Jack, 156–57
macomas, 20
    Bent-Nose Macoma, 22–23

Indented Macoma, 22–23
Pacific Grooved Macoma, 22–23
White Sand Macoma, 22–23, 24, 34
Macoma
  indentata, 22–23
  nasuta, 22–23
  secta, 22–23, 24, 34
Macrocystis pyrifera, 60–61, 62
Mactromeris hemphillii, 36–37
Malibu, x, 4
Malibu Beach, 2
Mallard, 226–27
mammals, 11, 174–87
  birds that prey on, 222, 228
  Marine Mammal Protection Act, 140
  and red tides, 30, 144
mantle, 13, 28, 40
Marine Mammal Protection Act, 140
marine reserves, 7, 158
marine snails. *See* snails
marine worms. *See* worms
medusa stage (cnidarians), 11, 150
Megaptera novaeangliae, 184
Megastraea undosa, 98–99
Megathura crenulata, 84–85
Melannita perspicillata, 226–27
Membranipora membranacea, 68–69
Merganser, Red-Breasted, 226–27
Mergus serrator, 226–27
mermaid's purse, 172–73
Mexico, 1, 2, 50, 184, 200
microorganisms, 42, 58, 88
minus tides, 8
Modiolus capax, 74–75
mollusks
  birds that prey on, 210, 222, 224, 226, 228
  camouflage of, 146
  definition of, 12
  fish that prey on, 158, 168, 170
  polyplacophora, 80–81
  of rocky shores, 72–113
  of sandy beaches, 16–51, 68–69
  and the seafood industry, 8
  without shells, 108–13
  See also bivalves; gastropods
moonsnails, 54, 106
  Lewis's Moonsnail, 48–49
  Recluz's Moonsnail, 48–49
  Spiral Moonsnail, 50–51
Mopalia muscosa, 80–81

Moray Eel, California, 164–65
moss animals, 68
Murex, Festive, 102, 104–5
murex family, 104
mussel beds, 72–73, 76, 92, 122, 130, 208
mussels, 80
  Bay Mussel, 38, 72–75
  California Mussel, 38, 72–74
  collecting of, 72
  Fat Horse Mussel, 72, 74–75
  and hydroids, 58, 59
  predators of, 102, 130, 208
  Ribbed Mussel, 38–39
  and the seafood industry, 8
  See also mussel beds
Mya, Boring, 78–79
Myliobatis californicus, 50, 168–69
Mytilus
  californianus, 72–73
  edulis, 72–75
  species, 72–75

nautilus, 112
Nearshore Waters, 140–87
nematocysts, 11, 114, 150
Nettle, Sea, 150–51
neurotoxins, 144
Neverita
  helicoides, 50–51
  reclusiana, 48–49
Newport Bay Ecological Reserve, 230
Norrisia norrisi, 64–65
Nucella emarginata, 104–5, 110–11
Nudibranch
  Horned, 110–11
  Opalescent, 110–11
  Sea-Clown, 110–11
  See also Corambe, Frost-Spot; Sea Hare, California Brown; Spiny Doris, Black-Tipped
Numenius phaeopus, 212–13
Nuttall, Thomas, 20
Nuttallia nuttallii, 20–21

Ocenebra species, 102
Ocinebrina species, 102
Octopus bimaculoides, 112–13
octopuses, 10, 12, 152, 164
  Giant Pacific Octopus, 112
  Two-Spot Octopus, 112–13
Oglicottus maculosus, 138–39
Olive, Purple, 106–7

Olivella biplicata, 106–7
one-finger rule, 7, 114
Opal Eye, 136–37
Opalia species, 46, 116–17, 126
operculum, 13, 94, 101
Orcinus orca, 178
Osprey, 228–29
ossicles, 134
Osteichthyes, 11
Ostrea lurida, 76–77
otter, sea, 100
overfishing, 206
ovoviviparous, 166, 168
Oyster
    American, 76–77
    California, 76–77
    Pacific, 76–77
Oystercatcher, Black, 208–9
Oyster Drill, Atlantic, 102–3

Pachygrapsus crassipes, 128–29, 230
Pacific Fly Zone, 188
Paguridae, 5
Pagurus
    hirsutiusculus, 126–27
    samuelis, 126–27
pallial line (bivalves), 12–13, 28
pallial sinus (bivalves), 12–13, 28
Palos Verdes Peninsula, x, 1
Pandion haliaetus, 228–29
Pandora, 38–39
Pandora punctata, 38–39
Panuliris interruptus, 152–53
paralytic shellfish poisoning, 144
Parastichopus
    californicus, 134–35
    parvimensis, 134–35
    species, 108
Passerculus sandwichensis beldingi, 232–33
peeps (sandpipers), 214, 216
Pelagia colorata, 150
Pelecanus
    erythrorhynchos, 202–4
    occidentalis, 202–5
pelicans, 190, 192, 208, 222, 224
    California Brown Pelican, 202–5
    White Pelican, 202–4
Penitella penita, 78–79
periostracum, 13, 74
periwinkles, 10, 96, 104
    Checkered Periwinkle, 94–95
    Eroded Periwinkle, 94–95

Phalacrocorax auritus, 206–7
Phoca vitulina, 176–77
phoebes, 232
photosynthesis, 62, 142
Phragmatopoma californica, 118–19
phylums, definitions of, 11–12
Physeter macrocephalus, 178
phytoplankton, 142–45
Pickleweed, 230, 232
Piddock
    Flat-Tipped, 78–79
    Rough, 78–79
pinnipeds, 174, 176
Pipefish, Bay, 138–39
Pisaster ochraceus, 130–31
plankton, 142–47, 148
    animals that consume, 24, 36, 52, 114
    composition of, 32, 94
Platyodon cancellatus, 78–79
Platyrhinoidis triseriata, 166–67
pleopods, 56
Plover
    Black-Bellied, 218–19
    Semipalmated, 218–19
    Snowy, 218
    See also Golden-Plover, Pacific
Pluvialis
    fulva, 218–19
    squatarola, 218–19
Podiceps
    auritus, 220–21
    nigricollis, 220–21
Point Conception, x, 1, 92, 158, 160, 184
Point Loma, x, 1
Pollicipes polymerus, 122–23
pollution, 6–8
    and arthropods, 54, 122
    and birds, 190, 232
    and dolphins, 180
    and fish, 206
    and kelp, 60
    and mollusks, 30, 42, 46, 82
    and red tides, 144
polyplacophora, 80–81
polyps, 11, 50, 58, 148
polyp stage (cnidarians), 150
porpoises, 178
Poseidon, 178
primary producers, 142
Prototothaca
    laciniata, 12, 32–33
    staminea, 32–33, 34

Pteropurpura festiva, 104–5
Pugettia producta, 66–67

radula, 46, 48, 82
Rail, Light-Footed Clapper, 230–31
Rallus longirostris levipes, 230–31
raptors, 228–29
rays, 11, 36, 54, 130, 188
    Bat Ray, 50, 168–69
    Thornback Ray, 166–67
rays (bivalves), 12–13
red tide, 8, 30, 72, 144–45, 228
refuge, wildlife, x, 230
reserves, ecological, 174, 189, 200, 230
reserves, marine, 7, 158
Rhinobatos productus, 166–67
Roach, Western Sea, 124–25
rock borers, 78–79
rock cod, 162
rockfish, 162
rocksnails, 102
Rocky Shores, 70–139
Roperia
    poulsoni, 102–3
    species, 102–3
Rynchops niger, 200–201

sagittal crest, 174
Salema, 156–57
Salicornia virginica, 230, 232
salp, 142, 146–47
Salpa species, 146–47
sand collar, 50–51
sand crab. *See* crabs
sand dollars, 12, 16, 120, 132, 134
    Sand Dollar, 52–53
Sanderling, 214–15, 216
San Diego, 2, 71
sandpipers, 190, 208–17, 218, 222
    Least Sandpiper, 216–17
    Western Sandpiper, 216–17
sandworms, 210, 211
Sandy Beaches, 16–69
San Elijo Ecological Reserve, 230
San Francisco, 174
San Pedro, 2, 124
Santa Barbara, x, 2, 174
Santa Catalina, x
Santa Cruz, 100
Santa Monica State Beach, x, 4, 17
Savannah Sparrow, Belding's, 232–33

Saxidomus nuttalli, 28–29, 36
Scallop
    Kelpweed, 44–45, 66
    Pacific Calico, 42–43
    Reddish, 42–43
    Rock, 44–45
scaup, 226–27
Scorpaena guttata, 162–63
Scorpaeniformes, 162
Scorpionfish, California, 162–63
Scoter, Surf, 226–27
Sculpin, Tidepool, 138–39
sea cucumbers, 12, 108
    California Sea Cucumber, 134–35
    Warty Sea Cucumber, 134–35
seagulls. *See* gulls
Sea Hare, California Brown, 108–9
seahorse, 138
sea lions, 11, 164, 176
    California Sea Lion, 174–75
    predators of, 170
    prey of, 152, 160
    and red tides, 72
seals, 11, 72, 152, 170, 180
    Harbor Seal, 176–77
Sea Nettle, 150–51
sea otter, 100
Sea Roach, Western, 124–25
sea slugs, 12, 68, 108–11, 134
sea stars, 10, 94, 132
    Bat Star, 130–31
    body structure of, 12, 52
    Ochre Sea Star, 130–31
    Pacific Sea Star, 130–31
    prey of, 72
sea urchins, 12, 52, 132–33, 134, 158
seaweed, 16, 72, 112, 118
    See also kelp
Sebastes serriceps, 162–63
Semicossyphus pulcher, 158–59
Sequit Point, 4
Serpula Columbiana, 118–19
Serpulorbis squamigerus, 46, 66–67, 118
Sertularella species, 58–59
sharks, 180
    classification of, 11
    eggs of, 62
    Great White Shark, 170, 186
    Horn Shark, 170–71
    Leopard Shark, 172–73
    prey of, 50, 54, 152, 176

and red tides, 144
Swell Shark, 172–73
Sheephead, California, 158–59
shellfish harvesting, 8, 26, 30, 72, 144
shells
composition of, 38
growth of, 38
identification of, 12–14
Shoveler, Northern, 226–27
shrimp, 162
Silver Strand State Beach, 216
Sinum scopulosum, 50–51
siphon. *See* clams
Skimmer, Black, 200–201
slippersnails, 16
Giant Slippersnail, 90–91
Hooked Slippersnail, 90–91
Onyx Slippersnail, 90–91
See also Half-Slipper, Pacific
slugs, sea. *See* sea slugs
snails, 10, 120
California Horn Snail, 46–47, 66, 230
drill, 72, 94
eggs of, 92
living on kelp, 64–67
Norris Top Snail, 64–65
Olive Snail, 106
predators of, 112, 190
of rocky shores, 82–107
of sandy beaches, 46–51
Scaly Tube Snail, 46, 66–67, 118
shelter for, 62, 72
See also moonsnails; slippersnails
Snapper, Pacific Red, 162
Solen rostriformis, 24–25
Spanish Shawl, 110–11
Sparrow, Belding's Savannah, 232–33
Spartina foliosa, 230
spider crab family, 152
Spiny Doris, Black-Tipped, 110–11
spiracles, 166
Spirorbis species, 118–19
sponges, 92, 110, 160, 208
squid, 112, 174
starfish. *See* sea stars
stars. *See* sea stars
Sterna
antillarum, 198–99, 219
caspia, 196–97
elegans, 196–97
forsteri, 198–99
maxima, 196

stinging cells, 11, 114, 148, 150
Stingray, Round, 168–69
stingray shuffle, 140, 168, 169
stomach-foot, 46
Strongylocentrotus
franciscanus, 132–33
purpuratus, 132–33
subtidal zone, 8, 10
Surfbird, 212–13
Surfclam, Hemphill's, 36–37
Surfperch, Barred, 156–57, 162
Sweetwater Marsh National Wildlife
Refuge, x, 230
Syngnathus leptorhynchus, 138–39

Tagelus
California, 24–25
Purplish, 24–25
Tagelus
californianus, 24–25
divisus, 24–25
Tattler, Wandering, 208–10
Tegula
brunnea, 96–97
eiseni, 96–97
funebralis, 96–97
tegulas, 98, 104, 126
Banded Tegula, 96–97
Black Tegula, 96–97
Brown Tegula, 96–97
Tellin, Bodega, 24–25
Tellina bodegensis, 24–25
Tellinidae, 5
telson, 56
terns, 192, 194, 200
Caspian Tern, 196–97
Elegant Tern, 196–97
Forster's Tern, 198–99
Least Tern, 198–99, 219
Royal Tern, 196
tests, 52, 132, 133
Tetraclita rubescens, 120–21
thorn drupe, 102
threatened species, 219, 228
tidepools, 7, 9, 70–71
tides, 8, 10, 154
See also red tide
tide table, 17
Tivela stultorum, 26–27
Tongva tribe, 82, 170

top shells, 96
  Blue Top Shell, 98
  Queen Top Shell, 98
  Western Ribbed Top Shell, 98–99
top spire (gastropods), 13–14
towhees, 232
Trachurus symmetricus, 156–57
Trachycardium quadragenarium, 34–35
Treefish, 162–63
Tresus nuttallii, 36–37
Triakis semifasciata, 172–73
Triopha catalinae, 110–11
Triton, Poulson's Dwarf, 102–3
tube worms. *See* worms
tunicates, 146–47, 208
turbans, 96
  Wavy Turban, 98–99
Turnstone
  Black, 208–9
  Ruddy, 208
Tursiops truncatus, 178–81

umbilicus (gastropods), 13–14, 96
unicorn shell, 102–3, 126, 127
univalves, 12, 46–51, 66, 82–107
urbanization, 2, 30, 219
  See also habitat loss
urchins, sea, 12, 52, 134, 158
  Red Urchin, 132–33
  Purple Urchin, 132–33
Urobatis halleri, 168–69
Urosalpinx
  cinerea, 102–3
  species, 102

varix (varices), 14, 100
Velella velella, 148–49
veliger, 26, 32
Veneridae, 5

Venice Beach, x, 2, 141, 200
Ventura Harbor, x
Venus clams, 22, 34
  California Venus, 30–31
  Pacific White Venus, 28–29
  Smooth Venus, 30–31
  Wavy Venus, 30–31, 32
Venus family, 26, 28
Vulture, Turkey, 228–29

warblers, 232
Wentletrap, 46, 116–17, 126
wetlands, coastal, 16, 188–89, 216
whales, 1, 11, 120, 142
  Blue Whale, 184
  Gray Whale, 178, 184–87
  Humpback Whale, 184
  Killer Whale, 178, 186
  Sperm Whale, 178
Whelk, Kellet's, 13, 100–101, 102
Whimbrel, 212–13
whorls, 13–14
Widgeon, American, 226–27
wildlife refuges, x, 230
Willet, 210–11
worms, 72, 166, 168, 212, 216
  Calcareous Tube Worm, 118–19
  Sandcastle Worm, 118–19
  spiral-tube, 118–19
  See also sandworms
wracks. *See* kelp

Xenistius californiensis, 156–57

Zalophus californianus, 174–75
Zirfaea pilsbryi, 78–79
zooids, 68
zooplankton, 142, 144

We encourage you to patronize your local bookstores. Most stores will order any title that they do not stock. You may also order directly from Mountain Press by mail, using the order form provided below or by calling our toll-free number and using your VISA, MasterCard, Discover, or American Express. We will gladly send you a complete catalog upon request.

Some other titles of interest:

_____	Coastal Wildflowers of the Pacific Northwest	$14.00
_____	Finding Fault in California: *An Earthquake Tourist's Guide*	$18.00
_____	Geology Underfoot in Death Valley and Owen's Valley	$18.00
_____	Geology Underfoot in Southern California	$14.00
_____	An Introduction to Northern California Birds	$14.00
_____	An Introduction to Southern California Birds	$14.00
_____	An Introduction to Southern California Butterflies	$22.00
_____	Loons: *Diving Birds of the North* (children)	$12.00
_____	Nature's Yucky: *Gross Stuff that Helps Nature Work* (children)	$10.00
_____	Owls: *Whoo Are They?* (children)	$12.00
_____	Roadside Geology of Northern and Central California	$20.00
_____	Roadside History of California	$20.00
_____	Roadside Plants of Southern California	$14.00
_____	Weather Extremes of the West	$24.00

Please include $3.00 per order to cover shipping and handling.

Send the books marked above. I enclose $_____

Name_____

Address_____

City/State/Zip_____

☐ Payment enclosed (check or money order in U.S. funds)

Bill my: ☐ VISA   ☐ MasterCard   ☐ Discover   ☐ American Express

Expiration Date:_____

Card No._____

Signature_____

Mountain Press Publishing Company
P. O. Box 2399 • Missoula, Montana 59806
Order Toll Free 1-800-234-5308
e-mail: info@mtnpress.com • web site: www.mountain-press.com

About the Author

A descendant of Spanish settlers and the Gabrieleno-Tongva tribe, **Marina Curtis Tidwell** has deep roots in coastal California. She grew up a few steps from Fisherman's Wharf in Monterey; has lived near the beach in Carmel, Coronado, San Diego, San Francisco, and Los Angeles; and has been a dedicated beach bum from the time she could walk. She is a speaker for Heal the Bay, a docent with the Santa Monica Pier Aquarium, and an avid bird-watcher who writes for the magazine *Birding Business*. Marina has a degree in filmmaking from the University of Southern California, and her wildlife photographs have appeared in Windstar Wildlife Institute publications among others. Marina and her husband, Robert, often take their three children to the beach, from San Pedro to Malibu, to study marine wildlife.